Supporting the Wounded Educator

Educators today are facing challenges and demands like never before. The tensions between an educator's calling and the reality of the profession can create a growing sense of compassion fatigue, burnout, and job dissatisfaction. In light of this context, this book brings firsthand knowledge alongside research to encourage, equip, and empower teachers and other K–12 educators to find relief and hope. Taking a trauma-sensitive approach, this important resource will help you navigate the pressures of being an educator, whether you entered into your profession carrying wounds with you, have felt wounded from your work environment, or you are simply someone trying to support others. Packed with doable strategies and suggestions for personal and professional self-care, this book will help you discover a personal journey toward holistic health, job satisfaction, and most importantly, hope!

Dardi Hendershott is co-founder of Hope 4 The Wounded, an organization committed to encouraging, equipping, and empowering schools and communities to reach children who are beyond "at-risk." Hope 4 The Wounded offers practitioner-based training across the globe about social/emotional literacy, empathy, inclusive communities, self-care and combating compassion fatigue, and other topics relevant to today's educational climate that help educators, leaders, and other child service professionals understand and reach wounded children.

Joe Hendershott has an extensive background working with at-risk and wounded youth as a teacher and administrator in traditional, alternative, and correctional education settings. He has been a high school assistant principal, head principal, alternative school principal, and a principal in a residential treatment facility. In 2006, he co-founded Hope 4 The Wounded with his wife, Dardi, and is a sought-after speaker and professional development trainer for trauma-informed practices and social emotional literacy.

Other Eye on Education Books Available from Routledge

(www.routledge.com/eyeoneducation)

7 Ways to Transform the Lives of Wounded Students
Joe Hendershott

Reaching the Wounded Student
Joe Hendershott

Becoming a Transformative Leader: A Guide to Creating Equitable Schools
Carolyn M. Shields

Bringing Innovative Practices to Your School: Lessons from International Schools
Jayson W. Richardson

Working with Students that Have Anxiety: Creative Connections and Practical Strategies
Beverley H. Johns, Donalyn Heise, and Adrienne D. Hunter

Implicit Bias in Schools: A Practitioner's Guide
Gina Laura Gullo, Kelly Capatosto, and Cheryl Staats

Five Practices for Improving the Success of Latino Students: A Guide for Secondary School Leaders
Christina Theokas, Mary L. González, Consuelo Manriquez, and Joseph F. Johnson Jr.

Leadership in America's Best Urban Schools
Joseph F. Johnson, Jr., Cynthia L. Uline, and Lynne G. Perez

Leading Learning for ELL Students: Strategies for Success
Catherine Beck and Heidi Pace

Supporting the Wounded Educator

A Trauma-Sensitive Approach to Self-Care

Dardi Hendershott and Joe Hendershott

NEW YORK AND LONDON

First published 2020
by Routledge
52 Vanderbilt Avenue, New York, NY 10017

and by Routledge
2 Park Square, Milton Park, Abingdon, Oxon, OX14 4RN

Routledge is an imprint of the Taylor & Francis Group, an informa business

© 2020 Joe Hendershott and Dardi Hendershott

The right of Dardi Hendershott and Joe Hendershott to be identified as authors of this work has been asserted by them in accordance with sections 77 and 78 of the Copyright, Designs and Patents Act 1988.

All rights reserved. No part of this book may be reprinted or reproduced or utilized in any form or by any electronic, mechanical, or other means, now known or hereafter invented, including photocopying and recording, or in any information storage or retrieval system, without permission in writing from the publishers.

Trademark notice: Product or corporate names may be trademarks or registered trademarks, and are used only for identification and explanation without intent to infringe.

Library of Congress Cataloging-in-Publication Data
Names: Hendershott, Dardi, author. | Hendershott, Joe, author.
Title: Supporting the wounded educator : a trauma-sensitive approach to self-care / Dardi Hendershott, Joe Hendershott.
Identifiers: LCCN 2019047125 (print) | LCCN 2019047126 (ebook) | ISBN 9780367415150 (hardback) |
ISBN 9780367429287 (paperback) |
ISBN 9781003000181 (ebook)
Subjects: LCSH: Teachers--Job stress. | Teachers--Mental health. | Teachers--Health and hygiene. | Teaching--Psychological aspects. | Stress management. | Well-being.
Classification: LCC LB2840.2 .H36 2020 (print) | LCC LB2840.2 (ebook) |
DDC 371.1001/9--dc23
LC record available at https://lccn.loc.gov/2019047125
LC ebook record available at https://lccn.loc.gov/2019047126

ISBN: 978-0-367-41515-0 (hbk)
ISBN: 978-0-367-42928-7 (pbk)
ISBN: 978-1-003-00018-1 (ebk)

Typeset in Palatino LT Std
by Cenveo® Publisher Services

This book is dedicated to every Warrior of Hope fighting the good fight to find hope for themselves and hope for the children who need it most.

> *"It doesn't concern me if what I do raises the eyebrows of a few;*
> *I am concerned if what I do makes a difference."*
>
> **~Dardi Hendershott**

Contents

Preface

On an extremely cold, blustery winter morning in early 2004, I received a phone call from Joe, who was serving as an assistant high school principal at the time. He choked out the words, "One of my students was killed in a car accident this morning," between sobs. This young lady was not only one of Joe's students but was also our then preschool-aged son's favorite people to see when we visited Daddy at work, and suddenly her light was gone. Everyone, including my husband, was scrambling to put support services into place for grieving, overwhelmed classmates. As I listened to my husband trying to gather himself in the corner of the auto body shop of the school, I had to wonder, "What about the adults? Who is helping the staff through this tragedy?"

Joe has spoken all over the world about working with wounded children. Time and again, we have both been approached with the question, "What about the wounded educators?" Sometimes this question was rooted in concerns for self; other times, it was the desperate plea for how to come alongside a struggling colleague. We have been reminded that many educators enter the school building with their own unresolved wounds or experience wounds in their current world that will impact their professional life, while others are valiantly trying to maintain a sense of morale and an emotionally safe workplace where students and adults alike can thrive. We recently went back through 100 submissions through our online course to examine the answer to one specific question regarding areas participants felt they needed to focus on strengthening. Of those submissions, seventy-one percent of participants stated that being aware of self-care and compassion fatigue was one of their biggest areas of need. One participant stated in her response,

> EVERY year, usually in October/November (between Parent/Teacher Conference time and Thanksgiving break) I start to show signs of compassion fatigue. This past year was particularly difficult, and I was not being very effective in the classroom. Our district has started paying some attention to teacher self-care. I started to take some steps in December to address my compassion fatigue, which was made worse by depression and anxiety resurfacing. I thought to myself, "How can I help my students (mostly at-risk, some I would classify as wounded) if I can't get a handle on my own situation?" I was not at my best for ME, let alone my students. I realize that I have to continue to take care of me and ask for help so that I can be 100% for my students. By doing this, I am modeling for my students that it's okay to ask for help. Asking for help is a sign of strength, not weakness as so many think.
>
> –Lisa H. from Iowa

Educators today are facing challenges and demands like never before. The likelihood of students having experienced some type of trauma in their lives is higher than it has ever been, children's access to technology and social media are on the rise, the instances of childhood anxiety and depression have increased, the suicide rate among adolescents is at an all-time high, school shootings and violence are in the back of everyone's mind, and high-stakes testing is taking its toll on students and teachers alike. These are but a few of the things that can overwhelm the most seasoned of professionals. Educators and youth service professionals face a vastly different reality in today's classrooms and communities than most were prepared for while earning their credentials in college. The tensions between their calling and the reality of their profession can create a growing sense of compassion fatigue, burnout, and job dissatisfaction, sometimes culminating in exiting their chosen professions altogether. With this growing concern in mind, we decided to embark on this journey to discover HOPE in the middle of the mess.

It has always been our belief that most people go into education with the desire to share their passions, knowledge, and abilities to prepare the next generation to become the best version of themselves in order to make a positive impact in this world. It is our hope that in the pages of this book, you might find validation through the acknowledgment of the obstacles, a better understanding of self and others, some practical ideas for self-care and increasing cultural morale, and most importantly, a reignited sense of purpose, determination, and passion to keep doing the hardest, most important job there is: Preparing young minds to be our hope for tomorrow.

Who Is This Book For?

This book references "teacher and educator" throughout, but it is applicable to any school personnel, school leadership, educational support persons, social workers, and any other child advocate professional, so please feel free to use the title of your professional position interchangeably within the text. In addition, you'll find at the end of this Preface as well as each chapter a section called "Reading, Reflection, and Discussion Points." We invite you to utilize the questions individually or in a group study as a springboard to healthy conversation. The information in this book is not intended as a substitute for counseling and/or advice from a trained medical health professional for specific diagnosis or treatment.

An Overview from Joe

It has been said that people typically have one of two reactions to a crisis situation: There are those who run to the scene of the crisis, and those who would just as soon get away from it as fast as they can. It is well known in my family and friendship circles, and I have no shame in admitting, that I can be found in the group of folks who would just as soon get away from crisis situations as quickly as possible, especially the medical kind. My wife, on the other hand, goes sprinting into any adverse circumstance like it's her job, whether it involves someone in our family or a complete stranger involved in some type of injury or accident. It wasn't long ago that our twenty-three-year-old son found himself on the side of the road in Florida with a blown tire (mind you, we live in Ohio). You guessed it, he called Mom.

Given my aversion to crisis situations, my chosen profession as an educator is a bit ironic, isn't it? Whether your role is teacher, administrator, school counselor, or support staff, at any given moment in the education field you can find yourself in the midst of a medical crisis, a safety crisis, an emotional crisis…the list is long, and we have no choice but to lean into crisis situations, sometimes as a first responder. For many of us when we first felt the call to becoming an educator, we never imagined the toll being in this profession would take on our own relationships, our mental health and wellness, and/or our physical health. Dardi and I set out to write this book together, not because we are counselors or therapists, but because we are choosing to go to the scene of a very real crisis: Educators are overwhelmed and are losing hope, and in turn, we are losing these gifted professionals. Dardi and I have navigated many years in the trenches of education as a tandem, and it's our desire to bring some of that firsthand knowing alongside some research to encourage, equip, and empower educators to find relief from feelings of hopelessness and helplessness.

The first chapter of the book is a look at the definitions of vicarious trauma/secondary trauma, compassion fatigue, and burnout as well as some research that assists in understanding the problem. If you've ever read one of my books about reaching wounded children, you'll note that the very first step is understanding. I hold this as truth to any type of dilemma:

You cannot be in a position to experience transformation without understanding the root of the problem, so understanding is exactly where we're going to start.

In the next chapter, we will talk about the wounded educator. Whether you entered into your profession carrying wounds with you, have felt wounded from your work environment, or you are simply someone trying to be a support to others, we will discuss the origination and repercussions of wounds to increase our personal understanding of potential triggers and challenge points that may be impeding relationships, job performance, job satisfaction, and quite possibly any attempts we make at self-care.

In the third chapter, we will move from understanding the problem into some action steps. I have found that the best place to start is with these questions: "Who are you trying to change? What are you trying to change? Why are you trying to change these things?" While the answers may seem obvious, I think they are worth investigating because if we don't have a solid sense of direction, we'll go nowhere fast.

Finally, we're going to dive into some doable strategies and suggestions for personal and professional self-care that impact not only you, but your organization. In Chapter 4, we will discuss some suggestions for self-care that go beyond temporary indulgences to positive habits that can position us for building resilience. In addition, it is our firm belief that cultivating cultures of empathic connections will serve us well as we seek to find purpose and fulfillment in our work, so we're going to see what that looks like along with the role each of us plays in carrying it out through Chapter 5's professional self-care strategies.

Ultimately, it is our desire that the pages of this book help in reigniting a soul that has hit the wall of despair. The reality is that we live in a broken world, but as educators, we have the capacity to bring hope into hopeless situations, but only if we attune to ourselves and to one another with a common vision for what can be.

Reading, Reflection, and Discussion Points

1. Have you experienced any crisis situations as an educator? If so, was there a response plan and/or support system in place? How did this crisis make you feel? How did you process those feelings?
2. Does your current organization have a response plan and support system in place should a crisis occur?
3. How have you defined self-care up to this point?
4. Do you currently incorporate any self-care into your life? If so, what does that look like? Has it been helpful?
5. What is your vision and hope for yourself? (You will get the opportunity to revisit this throughout the book, but take some time to consider it now and jot down some initial thoughts.) How about for your professional setting?

Acknowledgments

To every teacher, administrator, school counselor, social worker, CASA, guardian ad litem, judge, and so many others passionate about people and child welfare we've known over these many years: Thank you for answering our never-ending questions, for sharing your experiences, for entrusting us with your struggles or frustrations, and for processing so many thoughts and ideas with us. You are an integral part of everything we do.

To Our Children: You have been and continue to be the greatest blessings in our lives. Your love for others inspires us to keep striving in what we do. Thanks for your patience and encouragement throughout this process; this took lots of teamwork! We love you.

To Katie: Thank you for your willingness to share so that others would be encouraged by your story.

From Joe: Some of you have read my previous books about working with wounded students, but you'll note this book lists another author: my wife, Dardi. I'm not even sure where to start. This book is a reflection of two people who believe every person should have HOPE. Dardi, your determination and fortitude with research and getting our thoughts, research, and ideas from our heads and hearts to print has been amazing. Your desire to support those who work in hard places and difficult situations runs deep. Thanks for being who you are and for your willingness to share from a place of experience and authenticity. It's an honor to be in this together. Love you lots.

From Dardi: I appreciate every one of you who has inspired me with your knowledge, your stories, and/or given me the hard nudge to be authentic about my own wounds without fear or shame and made me feel like I have something important to say. I can only hope I've made you feel the same. To my husband: This is one crazy life. I never would have guessed a joint venture in the form of a book would be part of it, but I guess I shouldn't be surprised by much anymore. Thanks for the iced coffees just when I needed them and for this ongoing life adventure. I love you.

Meet the Authors

Dardi Hendershott, co-founder of Hope 4 The Wounded, LLC, is a self-proclaimed graduate of the school of hard knocks with a degree in finding HOPE. Along with her administrative role, Dardi is a trained and formerly licensed foster/adoptive parent and is a huge advocate for professionals working with children of trauma. Her own experiences as an adoptive mother and years of walking alongside Joe through the trials and tribulations of teaching and education administration give her a unique perspective to the demands placed on professionals serving wounded children that she has shared at educational conferences, with faith-based audiences, and with education majors at universities. Her passion is to equip, empower, and encourage those in the trenches each and every day with HOPE.

Joe Hendershott, Ed.D., founder of Hope 4 The Wounded, LLC, has an extensive background working with at-risk and wounded youth as a teacher, coach and administrator in traditional, alternative and correctional education settings. Hendershott has served as a high school assistant principal, head principal, alternative school principal and principal at a residential facility.

An in-demand speaker at international and national conferences, Hendershott offers training and professional development to schools and communities about understanding and working with wounded students, the effects of trauma on learning and behavior, emotional literacy, leadership, empathy, esteem, inclusive communities, and combating compassion fatigue.

He is the author of two books: *Reaching the Wounded Student* and *7 Ways to Transform the Lives of Wounded Students*. He is also the recipient of the National Crystal Star Award, which recognizes a leader in dropout prevention and intervention as well as the Raymond W. Bixler Award, which recognizes excellence in education.

Hendershott holds a bachelor's degree in education from The Ohio State University. He also earned a master's in school administration and a doctorate in leadership studies from Ashland University.

1

Secondary Trauma: The Struggle Is Real

We were licensed foster parents for several years. One day, Dardi left with our foster daughter to attend a scheduled parent visitation at the child services agency only to return many hours later with not one, but three little girls in tow. While sitting in the waiting room, she was approached by a social worker asking if we would be willing to accept a temporary, emergency placement of two little girls diagnosed with neglect and failure to thrive. Dardi, being Dardi, agreed. When the court appointment finally came well after dark, the children were transported from the hospital emergency room to where my wife was waiting with the van. The social worker quickly transferred two car seats, one containing a six-month-old and the other a two-year-old, from the county car into my wife's vehicle so she could get everyone on their way. Each child was tucked into their respective car seat under a blanket, and Dardi recalls giving each baby a quick kiss on the forehead before buckling in for the drive home. When she finally arrived home and unloaded the babies, what she saw underneath those blankets will forever be imprinted on her heart and mind. There are no words to describe their physical condition or the blank look in their eyes. To this day, she cannot speak about it without a catch in her throat and tears in her eyes.

This is what secondary (sometimes referred to as vicarious) trauma looks like, and for most educators, the details might be different, but the tragic stories and circumstances are on repeat with new names and new faces every single school year. As children enter our school buildings carrying with them their adverse experiences and wounds, we cannot help but be impacted by them. At the same time, these very children whose stories break our hearts can also be the source of frustration as we try to find creative pathways around the often negative attitudes and behaviors rooted in their stories. Our relationships with these wounded students can feel like a never-ending emotional obstacle course.

Over the years, we've come across a multitude of definitions for secondary trauma, vicarious trauma, compassion fatigue, and burnout. Early on, most definitions were geared toward professionals in the medical and mental health fields as well as social workers. The realization has finally come that we must acknowledge the validity of these experiences within the scope of education. For the purposes of this book, we have narrowed down the definitions that seem most applicable within the context of educational environments.

According to the National Child Traumatic Stress Network (n.d.), secondary trauma is defined as:

> ...the emotional duress that results when an individual hears about the firsthand trauma experiences of another. Each year more than 10 million children in the United States endure the trauma of abuse, violence, natural disasters, and other adverse events. These experiences can give rise to significant emotional and behavioral problems that can profoundly disrupt the children's lives and bring them in contact with child-serving professionals.

> For therapists, child welfare workers, case managers, and other helping professionals involved in the care of traumatized children and their families, the essential act of listening to trauma stories may take an emotional toll that compromises professional functioning and diminishes quality of life. Individual and supervisory awareness of the effects of this indirect trauma exposure is a basic part of protecting the health of the worker and ensuring that children consistently receive the best possible care from those who are committed to helping them.

The very nature of an educator is to be influential and involved in the lives of their students, but what they don't typically tell you in your studies and preparation for being an educator is that the street of influence goes both ways. The return on our investment into young lives and minds is not always neat and tidy. Remen (1996) states, "The expectation that we can be immersed in suffering and loss daily and not be touched by it is as unrealistic as expecting to be able to walk through water without getting wet." If we are lucky, we get to see bits of success in the form of "light bulb" moments, growing confidence and esteem, the ever popular "good data," and so forth, but sometimes that return is in the form of a knowing and seeing that we didn't necessarily sign up for. Wounded children have lots of broken pieces. How many of you have picked up and carried a broken piece or twenty along the way for your students? We thought so. This is secondary trauma.

Compassion Fatigue

Unresolved secondary trauma can manifest itself as compassion fatigue. Merriam-Webster online defines compassion fatigue as "the physical and mental exhaustion and emotional withdrawal experienced by those who care for sick or traumatized people over an extended period of time." Simply stated by Dr. Charles R. Figley (1995), it is the "cost of caring" for others in emotional pain. Simply stated by Joe Hendershott, we're all in trouble, right? That's our reality folks: We are educators, we care, and the cost is high. Everywhere we speak, we pose two questions: How many of you are compassionate? How many of you are tired? In response to both questions, the majority of hands go up. Those broken pieces we pick up and carry can accumulate over time and become a load too heavy to bear, which leads us down the road of compassion fatigue. Figley further states, "We have not been directly exposed to the trauma scene, but we hear the story told with such intensity, or we hear similar stories so often, or we have the gift and curse of extreme empathy and we suffer. We feel the feelings of our clients. We experience their fears. We dream their dreams. Eventually, we lose a certain spark of optimism, humor and hope. We tire. We aren't sick, but we aren't ourselves" (1995).

Several years ago at a conference in Atlanta, Georgia, Joe decided to bring up compassion fatigue in one of his sessions. At the conclusion of the session, a woman who had been in education for thirty-six years approached him crying. She said the minute he started talking about compassion fatigue, she identified her struggle. She had confided in some people in her professional and friendship circles that she was feeling off and just didn't know what was wrong with her, but she became frustrated because everyone said she was burnt out. She said, "How can I be burnt out? I still have more to give. I still want to work, I still want to make a difference." We'll talk more about burnout in a bit, but therein lies a big difference. When individuals are experiencing compassion fatigue, they are indeed tired, but they tend to keep forging ahead, determined to keep doing what they do. Sadly, a person with compassion fatigue may still be performing, but the feelings of purpose, satisfaction, accomplishment, and joy are on the absence list. We don't want that, so let's start by looking at some possible indicators of compassion fatigue. Mind you, this is not an exclusive list, and *PLEASE*—we cannot emphasize this enough—*if you are experiencing any of these or other symptoms that may not be listed to an extreme that leaves you feeling debilitated, seek help from a professional.* There is absolutely no shame in consulting with an expert to overcome anything that is keeping you from living and experiencing life at its fullest.

Some of the indicators that might point to compassion fatigue:

- Physically or mentally/emotionally tired
- Overwhelmed by students' needs
- Overwhelmed by ordinary tasks
- Withdrawing or isolating
- Irritability over "small stuff"
- Pessimistic or cynical outlook regarding self, others, and/or situations
- Feelings of helplessness and hopelessness
- Blaming and/or complaining becomes the substance of most conversations
- Disrupted sleep
- Abusing drugs, alcohol, or food
- Difficulty concentrating
- A sense of dread or anxiety
- Increased absences or chronically late to work
- Inability to maintain balance of empathy and objectivity
- Expressions of low self-esteem and low self-worth

There are obvious reasons that we need to recognize and combat compassion fatigue on a personal level. None of us wants to live in a state of being that leaves us feeling depleted and without a hope and enthusiasm for our chosen profession. However, there's also a bigger picture reason we need to address compassion fatigue: indifference. Compassion fatigue left unaddressed can lead to indifference, and the more we've read and the more we've studied, we believe indifference is at the root of many societal ills, including the acts of violence that we are hearing about all too often in our schools and communities. Indeed, indifference may be the result of a sort of coping mechanism in the face of compassion fatigue, but if we desire that the young minds and hearts we influence on a daily basis have compassion and empathy, it is critical that we guard our own selves from reaching a tipping point that leads us to a place of being indifferent to our jobs and students, let alone our personal relationships. McDonald (2007) states:

> What is indifference? Where hope and hopelessness are full of emotion, indifference lacks it. Where hope and hopelessness often demand some kind of human action, indifference stifles it. Where hope and hopelessness are heartfelt, indifference has no heart. Where hope and hopelessness epitomize our deepest humanity, indifference diminishes it. Its qualities are carelessness, thoughtlessness, mindlessness, feelinglessness, and perhaps even, humanlessness. It is this diminished human state that creates the potential for personal and global catastrophe because indifferent people stand by idle and do nothing often with a callous and cowardice. Therefore, I suggest that one's state of indifference is an ignorant intersection of vacuity and numbness which reveals itself most conspicuously as apathy.

You might be thinking, "Whoa, guys, that's a bit extreme, isn't it?" No, it really isn't. We cannot tell you the number of times that people have told us they feel like they are growing numb to everything and everyone and just going through the motions. This is detrimental beyond words to humanity on the whole, but even more to the heart of an educator. Marlow states, "I discovered that compassion fatigue is a real thing. Emotions, so strong at first, can easily shift into apathy. The subsequent guilt is paralyzing; it can prevent us from ever doing anything and freeze us into inaction. No wonder some people live for themselves, unaware of or unengaged with those who desperately need help. When global problems overwhelm, the human tendency is to do nothing" (2016). Indifference robs an educator of the very essence of who they are and why they chose to teach and mentor young people: To make a difference, to possibly *be* the difference in their students' lives.

There are certain risk factors for compassion fatigue. By default, just being in the education profession where your life is intertwined for the better part of a day nine months out of the year with your students and their stories, you are at risk of experiencing a certain level of compassion fatigue at some point in your career. Teaching has been repeatedly characterized as being one of the most high stress occupations. According to one article listing, the 10 Most Stressful Jobs in America, teaching comes in at number four right between police officer and medical professional (Brinson, 2010). Other risk factors include both personal attributes and organizational, work-related stressors. Certain personalities are most susceptible to stress and compassion fatigue, including persons who are over conscientious, perfectionistic, and/or very giving of self. In addition, people prone to anxiety or depression may be at greater risk of experiencing compassion fatigue.

Burnout

We confess that years ago when we first started addressing compassion fatigue in educators, we would only touch on burnout briefly because certainly most teachers would not reach this point unless their compassion fatigue was left to run amok. In light of ongoing research on the topic, we stand corrected. Where compassion fatigue very much involves the heart and relationships, burnout tends to evolve due to the extraneous elements of teaching: High stakes testing, perceived lack of support from administration and society at-large, lack of autonomy, lack of appreciation, and heightened workload, to name a few.

In other words, burnout involves the organizational elements of the workplace. According to the Mayo Clinic (n.d.), some questions you can ask yourself to help identify burnout include:

- Have you become cynical or critical at work?
- Do you drag yourself to work and have trouble getting started?
- Have you become irritable or impatient with coworkers, customers, or clients (read: students)?
- Do you lack the energy to be consistently productive?
- Do you find it hard to concentrate?
- Do you lack satisfaction from your achievements?
- Do you feel disillusioned about your job?
- Are you using food, drugs, or alcohol to feel better or to simply not feel?
- Have your sleep habits changed?
- Are you troubled by unexplained headaches, stomach or bowel problems, or other physical complaints?

As you can see, some of the potential symptoms of burnout overlap with those of compassion fatigue. According to Boyle (2011), compassion fatigue and burnout are closely related, both associated with a sense of depletion. The primary difference is the driving force behind the feelings. Burnout typically stems from conflict or dissatisfaction in the workplace whereas compassion fatigue emerges from relational connections with those being cared for (students, parents, other family members, or friends). Generally, the response to burnout is withdrawal while those experiencing compassion fatigue tend to keep giving of themselves.

Friends, there is a harsh reality that many systems in place are upside down in education. They are a point of frustration and definite cause for concern as the number of educators exiting the profession continues to climb. We could cite statistic after statistic to confirm this as well as up the word count for this book, but it would feel like beating a dead horse. At the end of the day, this is what we know: Educators are doers. We want to be productive and constructive in our doing, so when something hinders that desire, it is frustrating. Bruer (2018) beautifully states, "While burnout obviously has something to do with stress, overdoing things, not being centered, and not listening to yourself or your body, one of the deepest contributors to burnout, I believe, is the deep disappointment of not living up to your true calling, which is to help."

Many contributing factors to experiencing secondary trauma, compassion fatigue, and burnout in our profession are things out of our control. Knowing and accepting this is hard, but if we move forward in the coming pages into things we can control, we can potentially find a more peaceful existence within the adversities that feel unjust or cumbersome.

Reading, Reflection, and Discussion Points

1. Have you experienced secondary trauma? If so, have you ever gone a year without experiencing secondary trauma? If you have not experienced secondary trauma, do you know of colleagues who have experienced it?
2. Is there a particular child/student who sticks out in your mind when you think of trauma? If so, what emotions do those thoughts evoke?
3. How would you describe compassion fatigue in your own words?
4. Do you identify with any of the indicators for compassion fatigue? If so, take a moment to note the ones that feel the most significant to you.
5. Have you ever considered the impact of indifference on society as a whole? In your own words, how do you believe the impact of indifference would be different than the impact of empathy on one's self and society?
6. Revisiting the questions posed by the Mayo Clinic contained in this chapter, do any of them strike a chord with you? If so, do

you think that the needs of students or the work culture contribute the most to your feelings? (There is no wrong answer here. By taking a moment to consider the root of feelings, it's easier to help identify compassion fatigue vs. burnout.) If you feel your answer is "both," how would you break your answer down into percentages?

7. When considering your personality, do you find yourself trying to control certain aspects of your professional environment more than others?
8. How do you think having an understanding of secondary trauma, compassion fatigue, and burnout might be beneficial to you personally as well as within your professional relationships?
9. As you revisit your vision and hope for yourself, what might you add or adjust after reading this chapter? What about for your professional setting?

References

Boyle, D. (Jan 31, 2011). Countering compassion fatigue: A requisite nursing agenda. *OJIN: The Online Journal of Issues in Nursing, 16*(1), Manuscript 2. DOI: 0.3912/OJIN.Vol16No01Man02.

Brinson, L. C. (2010). 10 Most Stressful Jobs in America. Retrieved January 2020, from https://money.howstuffworks.com/10-most-stressful-jobs-in-america.htm

Bruer, J. (2018). *Helping Effortlessly.* Victoria, BC, Canada: Tellwell Talent.

Figley, C. R. (1995). Compassion fatigue as secondary traumatic stress disorder: An overview. In C. R. Figley (Ed.), *Brunner/Mazel psychological stress series, No. 23. Compassion fatigue: Coping with secondary traumatic stress disorder in those who treat the traumatized* (pp. 1–20). Philadelphia, PA: Brunner/Mazel.

Marlow, C. (2016). *Doing good is simple; making a difference right where you are.* Grand Rapids, MI: Zondervan.

Mayo Clinic Staff. (n.d.) Job burnout: How to spot it and take action. Retrieved June 2019, from https://www.mayoclinic.org/healthy-lifestyle/adult-health/in-depth/burnout/art-20046642

McDonald, J. E. (2008). The spirit of hope and its near enemy indifference: a phenomenological continuum. *Probing the Boundaries of Hope*. Oxford, England: Inter-Disciplinary Press eBook.

Merriam-Webster Online Dictionary. (n.d.) Retrieved April 2019, from https://www.merriam-webster.com/dictionary/compassion%20 fatigue

Remen, R. N. (1996). *Kitchen table wisdom: Stories that heal.* New York, NY: Riverhead Books.

The National Child Traumatic Stress Network. (n.d.). Secondary traumatic stress. Retrieved April 2019, from https://www.nctsn.org/trauma-informed-care/secondary-traumatic-stress.

2

The Wounded Educator

Over a year ago, we had decided to move back home to Ohio after having spent a couple years residing in Florida. The house we found for our family happened to have a swimming pool, but we weren't completely sold on the idea of having one. Swimming pools require attention, maintenance, and let's face it, a swimming pool seems more appropriate for Florida's climate rather than Ohio's. However, the house was a good fit for our family, so the pool was just part of the package.

We moved at the very end of March, so we were able to ignore the pool for a couple of months, but the time came when we had to lift the cover to see what was going on underneath. We knew it wasn't going to be pretty because we had been informed during the purchase process that the pool had been neglected for a couple of years. Sure enough, it was a mess. We opened the cover to find what looked like a dark green abyss. The first inclination was to just put the cover back on and pretend it wasn't there, but that wasn't really going to solve anything, so we began the work of figuring out what to do with that mess.

Turns out we needed to fix the filter, we needed a professional to come in and help us get that water clear and balanced, and then we learned how to keep it balanced through lots of trial and error. If you don't keep things balanced, that nasty green stuff will overtake the whole thing all over again. It took some time, some effort, some help, and some intention, but at the end of the effort, there was a reward. The darn pool that we were reluctant to embrace now serves as a place of connection, a place of peace, a place of joy, and even a place of strength and freedom. One of our daughters has spina bifida, which makes certain physical activities more challenging for her. However, she has a newfound strength and freedom in that swimming pool.

Unpacking our wounds can feel counterintuitive, especially in a world where we like to keep things neat and tidy, avoiding anything that resembles discomfort. However, just like the swimming pool, if we don't take a look at what's underneath the cover, we'll never be able to assess what we may need to address to become the best version of ourselves. It takes some time, it takes some intention, it takes some patience, it takes some trial and error, and in some cases, it might require a professional, but acknowledging our wounds and the obstacles they create in how we see ourselves and interact with others is worth the effort. We can create a filter for our wounds so that instead of them being a constant source of pain, shame, and isolation, we can pour hope and truth into the dark places to find freedom, strength, and even connection because we will have the capacity to extend a deeper sense of empathy and compassion for others facing their own adversity.

We are asked often, "Why wounded?" "Trauma is the Greek word for 'wound.' Although the Greeks used the term only for physical injuries, nowadays trauma is just as likely to refer to emotional wounds. We now know that a traumatic event can leave psychological symptoms long after any physical injuries have healed" (Merriam-Webster online). Being trauma-informed has become somewhat of a gold standard in recent years, and unfortunately, it seems that we are becoming desensitized to it as just another educational buzzword. However, back in 2006, we began referring to children who have experienced trauma as being "wounded" to emphasize the significance of the negative impact traumatic events have on a child's development, relationships, behaviors, and how they view themselves within this world. We believe it's just as important for adults to not be desensitized to the realities of navigating one's own personal trauma, as well. Statistics confirm that a large majority of adults have experienced some type of traumatic event along the way. According to a fact sheet provided by the Post Traumatic Stress Disorder (PTSD) Alliance on the Sidran Institute website (n.d.), "An estimated 70 percent of adults in the United States have experienced a traumatic event at least once in their lives and up to 20 percent of these people go on to develop post-traumatic stress disorder, or PTSD." Brenner (2017) states in an article in *Psychology Today* that, "Adults who suffer from developmental trauma may go on to develop Complex Post Traumatic Stress Disorder, or 'cPTSD,' which is characterized by difficulties in emotional regulation, consciousness and memory, self-perception, distorted perceptions of perpetrators of abuse, difficulties in relationships with other people, and negative effects on the meaningfulness of life." Regarding the impact of trauma, Dr. Mark Goulston emphasizes, "Unlike simple stress, trauma changes your view of your life and yourself. It shatters your most basic assumptions about yourself and your world—'Life is good,' 'I'm safe,' 'People are kind,' 'I can trust others,' 'The future is likely to be good'—and replaces them with feelings like 'The world is dangerous,' 'I can't win,' 'I can't trust other people,' or 'There's no hope'" (2008).

Before we go any further, we'd like to address a couple of questions that come about often and that you may be wondering yourself at this point: Why is it that some people seem to handle adverse experiences with a high level of resilience while others are quite negatively impacted? Why do some people respond to adverse experiences with a determination to overcome while others seem to crumple? Just as we've encouraged educators to see wounded children as unique individuals, we'd like for us to do the same as we look at ourselves and others in our midst. Judging ourselves or others for their response to life's hard is only serving to create a barrier to relationships. Human beings are not created, nor do they operate in a cookie cutter fashion, so our responses to adversity will be as diverse as we are. We are complex in our feelings and reactions and have different levels of support systems in place, so to assume that everyone should respond in the same way to similar life experiences is just not realistic. We'd like to suggest that right here and right now we throw out any judgment cards we have on the table toward ourselves or toward others who are struggling in our midst. Brown states, "Owning our story and loving ourselves through the process is the greatest thing we will ever do. Owning our story can be hard but not nearly as difficult as spending our lives running from it. Embracing our vulnerabilities is risky but not nearly as dangerous as giving up on love and belonging and joy—the experiences that make us the most vulnerable. *Only when we are brave enough to explore the darkness will we discover the infinite power of our light.* The willingness to tell our stories, feel the pain of others, and stay genuinely connected in this disconnected world is not something we can do halfheartedly. To practice courage, compassion, and connection is to look at life and the people around us, and say, 'I'm all in'" (2010). Let's move forward without shame exploring the complicated, amazing people we are in spite of the obstacles and discover how our perceived areas of weakness might in fact be our greatest avenues to strength.

Understanding Wounds

In Joe's previous book *7 Ways to Transform the Lives of Wounded Students,* he shares information gleaned from Dr. Terry Wardle, a leading expert in the field of trauma and wounded behavior.

There's much information about the impact of trauma available, but we still find Dr. Wardle's typology of wounds (2007) beneficial not only as it pertains to wounded students, but people in general:

- *Wounds of withholding:* When a person's physical and/or emotional needs are unmet.
- *Wounds of aggression:* When a caregiver or trusted person has acted in a physically and/or emotionally abusive way to another person.
- *Wounds of stressful events:* When an uninvited event happens that is beyond what is considered normal in a person's life.
- *Wounds of betrayal:* When a caregiver or trusted person misuses or abuses their power with another person.
- *Wounds of long-term duress:* When a prolonged season of pressure or pain has a devastating effect on a person.

You'll note that all these wounds center around our core needs being taken care of, to be safe and feel secure, to trust, and to feel like the world around us makes sense. In a perfect family or ideal community, none of these things would ever be threatened or unfulfilled, but unfortunately that's not what this world looks like. As humans, we inevitably will disappoint one another, but wounds transcend disappointment to being a painful infliction upon a person that impairs future interactions with others, how they view themselves, and how they view the world around them.

We've included in the appendix of this book a Trauma Indicator Chart we initially created to assist school personnel in identifying wounds in children. You may find it useful in assessing the experiences you've had in your own personal journey. Some examples of wounds of withholding would be food and other basic needs, affection, healthy physical touch, affirmation/praise, attention, and so on (this is not an exhaustive list). Wounds of aggression can include both physical and mental types of abuse. Wounds of stressful events could include losing a caregiver through death or removal from the home as a child, witnessing violence, losing a home, witnessing an accident, etc. Again, this is not an exclusive list, and for some, what is profoundly distressing to one person might be mildly distressing to another and may not have the same effect long term. Wounds of betrayal can certainly overlap with other types of wounds. For example, a wound of aggression might also evoke feelings of betrayal, as well, if a person who should be keeping you safe from harm has instead inflicted harm. Wounds of betrayal can also arise out of broken promises and lies. Finally, wounds of long-term duress can stem from anything from dealing with a chronic or terminal illness to fighting addiction to being immersed in a toxic environment at home or work.

Regardless of the source, we believe the foundational piece to the effective implementation of self-care is acknowledging our woundedness. This is worth repeating, so let's sit with this idea for another minute: The foundational piece to the effective implementation of self-care is acknowledging our woundedness. In doing so, we've begun the journey to self-discovery, which ultimately allows us to know and attend to what we truly need in self-care to function as the best versions of ourselves.

Defining Our Personal Trauma

Hear us when we say this: Trauma is NOT a life sentence. To the contrary, adversity contextualized can be used to increase our capacities for attunement and resilience within our jobs and our relationships. May we suggest that instead of allowing trauma to negatively define us, we look at how we can redefine our thoughts about the trauma? By redefine, we *do not* mean minimize or discount. However, we absolutely believe we have the power and the fortitude to pour truth into any false beliefs derived from adversity and to view our experiences through a new lens, or "filter," of how they can strengthen, and at the very least not hinder, our interactions with ourselves and with others.

Dardi shares, "When I first met Joe many years ago, I carried a heavy load of hurt from having been in an abusive relationship. I liked pretending it didn't have any effect on me, when in all actuality, it felt like a hurdle I was always fighting to overcome. After we were married for several years, I was approached about facilitating a recovery group at our church. This thought intimidated me a great deal. Life was good. Joe and I were expecting another baby and I liked keeping that part of my life tucked away in the recesses of my mind. What would it be like to revisit all that stuff? What would people think of me? Reluctantly, I agreed. I will never forget the first night of group when Joe was helping me get people registered. A couple of women came in that knew of our family but didn't really know me. I remember one of them looked at me strangely, which in all honesty made me want to bolt the scene. Instead, I proceeded with getting group started and shared my story.

A couple weeks later, that same woman pulled me aside and said, 'I owe you an apology.' Completely puzzled, I asked her why. She went on to say, 'When I first saw you sitting there with your cute baby belly and your nice husband that first night at registration, I thought, 'What does she know about my life?' I almost left but then you shared your story. I could hardly breathe because you do know about my life. And now I see hope for myself because I see you survived.' I may have been the facilitator of that group, but in that moment, I learned a huge lesson. Nobody needs our perfection; people need real."

Does this mean we throw our whole life story into every single conversation? No, it doesn't. However, we don't hesitate when it's appropriate or helpful to someone else going through a rough time because we've come to peace with the fact that while there might be parts of our stories we don't like, it is a part of who we are. Our hardest experiences have given us a new perspective to appreciate that everybody has a story that needs understanding and compassion.

At this juncture, you may be getting a little antsy just wanting to get through the heavy lifting and onto the self-care strategies. We completely understand because this starts sounding like a lot of mental exercise, and that can feel overwhelming. Hang in there with us, and here's why: We mentioned before that time and time again we've had people approach us with, "What about the wounded educator?" so we need to have a conversation about wounds. We need to see where our experiences, as well as the resulting thoughts about those experiences, may be sabotaging any attempts at self-care we make. As much as we wanted to remove the pool cover and go straight to having crystal clear water overnight, it actually took much, much longer than that to get the pool to where we really needed it to be to serve us well. Revisiting our statement about acknowledging our woundedness being the foundational piece to implementing effective self-care, think of it this way: I can keep bandaging the wound on my foot, but if I don't acknowledge and tend to the splinter that is festering underneath, those bandages are a waste of time, energy, and resources. Going back to the swimming pool analogy, it would be like leaving the cover on the pool and expecting the water to clear up on its own, or worse yet, continually throwing a bunch of chlorine at it without addressing the overall picture wouldn't help either.

We don't know about you, but when it comes to making some changes, we like things broken down in a way that we can easily digest the information. There's so much amazing information out there regarding trauma; however, trying to make heads or tails of it all and how it can be applied on a personal level can be mind-boggling. In the spirit of simplicity, we've always utilized Dr. Wardle's typologies of wounds that were shared at the beginning of this chapter to help people understand the origination of wounds. We've also found that Dr. Wardle's description of the cycle of wounds is extremely helpful in identifying the obstacles unresolved trauma can create.

According to Wardle, the typical cycle of wounds (2007) is as follows (see Figure 2.1):

1. *Wound:* A traumatic event leaving a deep impact on a person's life experience.
2. *False beliefs:* The wound stirs up negative feelings in a person, which leaves them believing negative generalities about self and others.
3. *Emotional upheaval:* The wound and false beliefs can lead to anger, sadness, depression, shame, or other unsettled feelings.
4. *Dysfunctional behavior:* This occurs when people respond to their pain in negative, unhealthy ways.
5. *Life situations:* Unresolved past trauma impacts various aspects of life.

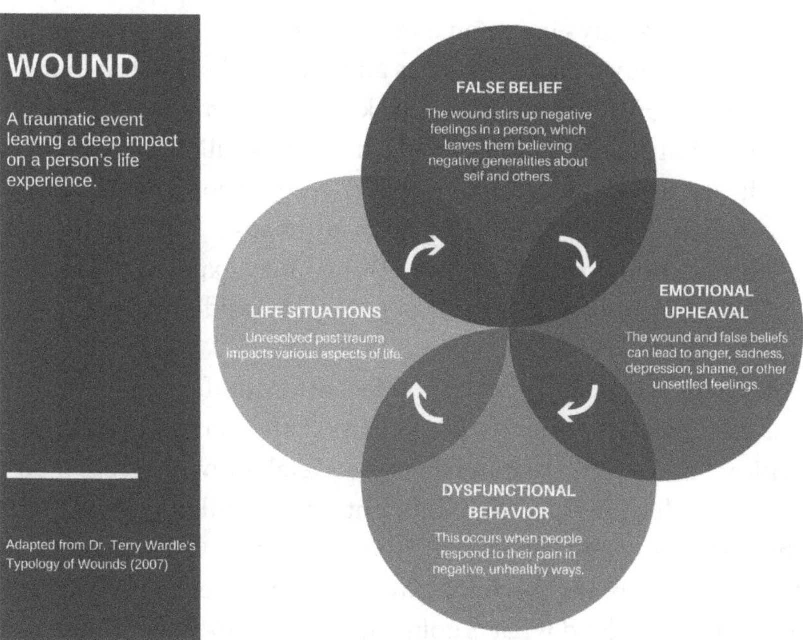

FIGURE 2.1 Cycle of wounds

Source: Adapted from Dr. Terry Wardle's Typology of Wounds (2007)

Unless you happen to be in that thirty percent of people who have been fortunate enough to not have had a significant traumatic event in their life, you can probably identify with some aspect(s) of Dr. Wardle's typology of wounds discussed in the previous section. If you are a visual person, you can see from the above chart how unresolved trauma can become a vicious cycle. In our house, we call this getting stuck on the emotional hamster wheel: Running in circles while going nowhere, never sure if we are running away from or chasing after something. As educators, we are working through this cycle of wounds with our students when in reality, we need to be sensitive to how it pertains to us, as well. Van der Kolk (2014) explains:

> ...what has happened cannot be undone. But what can be dealt with are the imprints of the trauma on body, mind, and soul: the crushing sensations in your chest that you label as anxiety or depression; the fear of losing control; always being on alert for danger or rejection; the self-loathing; the nightmares and flashbacks; the fog that keeps you from staying on task and from engaging fully in what you are doing; being unable to fully open your heart to another human being. Neuroscience research shows that the only way we can change the way we feel is by becoming aware of our inner experience and learning to befriend what is going on inside ourselves.

Does that last sentence make you feel as uncomfortable as it does us? As a male, it's easy for Joe to immediately fall into the stereotypical "dudes need to toughen up" societal norm, whereas others of us, Dardi being one, were brought up to "pull ourselves up by the bootstraps and get over it." None of these lines of thinking leaves any room for "becoming aware of our inner experience and learning to befriend what is going on inside ourselves." Right here and right now, we want to make it crystal clear that we already know what the result of stuffing the hard looks and feels like, and it isn't macho, nor does it make you a pillar of strength. In all actuality, it cuts you off at the knees, chews you up, and then spits you out into a heap of anger, anxiety, fear, or a multitude of other unhealthy and counter-productive mindsets. In other words, nothing good typically comes from just bucking up.

Once you've identified the wound(s) you carry, you can ask yourself:

1. What is my false belief?
    - *It was my fault.*
    - *No one cares about me.*
    - *I don't deserve _____. (love, happiness, care, etc.)*
    - *I must perform.*
    - *I'm not good enough/tall enough/small enough/smart enough/strong enough.*
    - *I don't matter.*
    - *(Fill in the blank)*
2. What does my emotional upheaval look like?
    - *Anger*
    - *Bitterness*
    - *Sadness*
    - *Anxiety*
    - *Depression*
    - *Constant frustration*
    - *Low self-esteem*
    - *Hopelessness*
    - *(Fill in the blank)*
3. What are my dysfunctional behaviors (remember, this is not about guilt, it's about vision)?
    - *Excessive eating*
    - *Alcohol or substance abuse*
    - *Excessive sleeping or other avoidant behavior*
    - *Isolation*

- *Attention seeking or neediness*
- *Constant complaining or gossiping*
- *Impulsive decisions*
- *(Fill in the blank)*

4. What are the resulting life situations (actual or potential)?

- *Impaired relationships*
- *Job dissatisfaction*
- *Loss of identity*
- *Emotional poverty*
- *Mental/physical illness*
- *(Fill in the blank)*

We would suggest that you take some time to process through these questions either in a journal or utilize the reading, reflection, and discussion guide at the end of the chapter. Even if none of these pertain to you personally, you might take time to reflect about someone you are close to or some of your students. If we seek to develop healthy communities of people, it can only serve us well to view others' situations and behaviors through a lens of understanding versus a lens of judgment or misunderstanding.

Repercussions of Wounds in the Workplace

Education is a people business. The social emotional component of education is finally being recognized as a critical piece to overall childhood development, and as educators, we are challenged with creating space for the students in our charge to experience self-discovery. So when will we allow humanization for ourselves? We must first acknowledge the beautiful and the messy of who we are and where we've been, and then we need to consider the wounds we've experienced and how they affect us.

When considering how our own adverse experiences have shaped us, we've developed a graphic to illustrate the Manifestation of Educator Wounds (MEW Chart) (see Figure 2.2) to expand on Dr. Wardle's cycle of wounds:

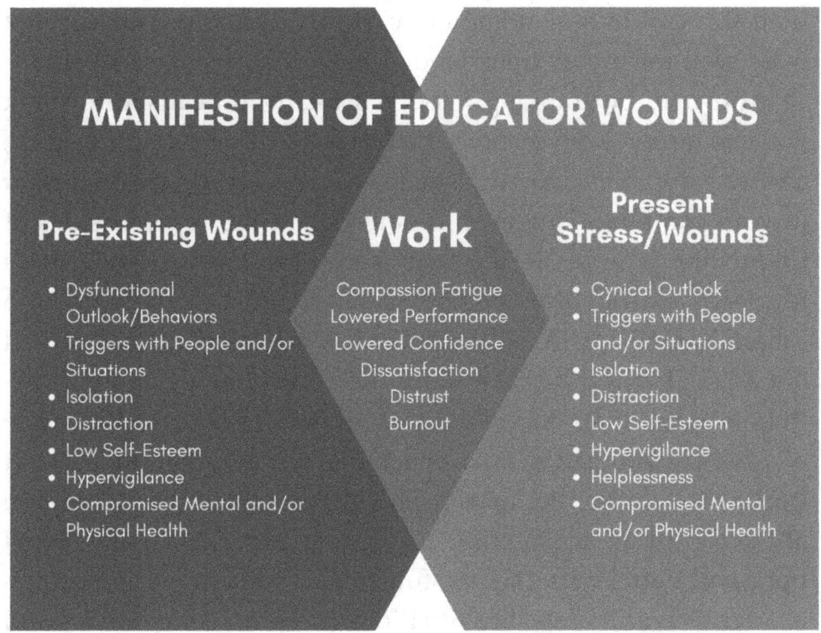

FIGURE 2.2 Manifestation of educator wounds

Whether we like it or not, this is our reality, folks. Our past intersects with our present right in the middle of our workplace. However, don't be daunted by this reality or feel like you are the only one. Looking back, Joe wishes he had understood how his own adverse experiences would impact not just his personal self, but his conduct in professional settings, as well.

Joe shares, "When I was fourteen years old, I walked into my home to find my dad holding a gun. He told me to take care of my brothers, my sister, and my mom. Somewhere between adrenaline and instinct, I took the gun away before anything happened. In my young mind, the question of 'what if?' was processed on repeat from that time on. Fast forward to adulthood where I became a dad and an educator. People would say often, 'You are so paranoid.' I would joke back saying, 'No, I'm just conscientious,' but I did find myself in a mode of always feeling like I needed to play defense against life, anticipating every single thing that could possibly go wrong whether it was with my children at home or with my students. This did not bode well for my anxious tendencies."

You may be thinking, "Joe, it's totally unrealistic to think you can, or are even responsible for, preventing bumps, bruises, and bad decisions in every single scenario," and you'd be right in your thinking. However, if you look at the repercussions of preexisting wounds in the chart above, you can see how Joe's fourteen-year-old brain processed that traumatic experience into a hard wiring for hypervigilance. His adolescence had carved out a belief that if he wasn't one step ahead at all times, something tragic would happen. If you go back to Dr. Wardle's cycle of wounds, you can easily unpack this whole situation and sort it into the wound, the false beliefs (I must be at the right place at the right time all the time to prevent a crisis), the emotional upheaval (anxiety), the dysfunctional behaviors (hypervigilance), and ultimately, life situations (keeping everyone around him uptight with his hypervigilance).

For many people, it comes naturally to view ourselves as the sum of our life experiences, and all too often, the sum feels like it's heavily in the negative. In "teacher speak," adversity seems to carry the highest score on a weighted grading scale. Scientifically, one article affirms this commonality stating, "Our capacity to weigh negative input so heavily most likely evolved for a good reason—to keep us out of harm's way. From the dawn of human history, our very survival depended on our skill at dodging danger. The brain developed systems that would make it unavoidable for us not to notice danger and thus, hopefully, respond to it" (Marano, 2003). In other words, our brains naturally process negative experiences more intentionally as a survival instinct, so this can be a good thing if we've learned to filter these experiences in a way that is advantageous in our everyday interactions. However, adverse experiences carry a lot of negative emotions that are not easily translated through a critical thinking lens. Instead, they become unaddressed wounds with detrimental repercussions (note that we will discuss counteracting these repercussions through various personal and professional self-care strategies in later chapters):

1. *Dysfunctional outlook/behaviors:* If we've had an adverse experience early in life, it tends to skew how we view the world, situations, people, and even ourselves. Instead of seeing the world as a relatively safe place to explore and discover, we tend to be suspect of everyone and everything. You'll note that in the right column of the MEW Chart, it says "Cynical Outlook" instead of dysfunctional. We believe, unfortunately, at some point a dysfunctional or unhealthy outlook can become cynical in nature. By definition, having a cynical outlook means one is "contemptuously distrustful of human nature and motives" (Merriam-Webster online). You can see how operating from this vantage point within the educational setting would be exhausting. Any student exhibiting disruptive behavior has the potential to trigger feelings of being personally attacked, whereas criticism from a colleague could likewise be received in the same manner resulting in unhealthy responses.
2. *Triggers with people and/or situations:* When adverse experiences leave a significant imprint on our sense of self and/or safety, certain scenarios can be a trigger resulting in feelings of shame, anger, fear, or being threatened. And let us tell you from experience, there's nothing like having a child in your midst with their own traumatic responses to unveil your own triggers. Having triggers does not make you weak or less than; it makes you human. However, it's imperative to recognize our triggers so we can respond in healthy ways we can feel good about later. For Joe, he can get uptight about a whole lot of things, but when a student started going off on him back in the day calling him every name he could think of out the open bus window,

he could separate himself from it. He was more curious about what set the student off on his tangent in the first place and was somewhat humored by the whole thing because it really came out of nowhere. Obviously, it had to be addressed because it wasn't appropriate behavior, but they had a nonconfrontational conversation about it at school the next day. Joe received an apology and the student received some time helping the administrative assistant with reorganizing her office. However, Joe had a colleague once who went into a full-blown tirade with a kid who called him a rather colorful explicative out of anger over a situation another student had initially escalated. Seriously, this situation went from zero to demanding expulsion in a matter of five seconds! Later, the teacher was mortified and said all he could hear was his dad screaming at him in that moment. Come to find out, he had endured years of verbal abuse. So here you have two people with two completely different responses to similar situations based on their life experiences. Knowing our triggers as educators can serve two purposes: (a) We work with children who have experienced trauma, so they struggle behaviorally often; if we know what our triggers are and can have practiced healthy responses in our arsenal, potentially confrontational situations can become teachable moments where we remain the calm, objective, and consistent authority figure, and (b) we avoid walking away from a situation feeling bad about how we handled it or like we contributed to its escalation instead of its de-escalation.

3. *Isolation:* When life has been hard, or if life is currently hard, isolation often masquerades itself as safety. Whether we fear shame, judgment, feeling vulnerable, or think avoiding people will somehow allow us to avoid our struggle, the truth is that people need people. We are designed to live in community, and in community is where we find resilience.

According to Perry and Szalavitz (2008), "Because humans are inescapably social beings, the worst catastrophes that can befall us inevitably involve relational loss. As a result, recovery from trauma and neglect is also all about relationships—rebuilding trust, regaining confidence, returning to a sense of security and reconnecting to love. Of course, medications can help relieve symptoms and talking to a therapist can be incredibly useful. But healing and recovery are impossible—even with the best medications and therapy in the world—without lasting, caring connections to others." Looking back at Dardi's story, this is a perfect example of where two individuals stepped away from the perceived security of their isolation to find healing and hope in their shared experiences.

4. *Distraction:* Life in general can be chaotic, so adding into the mix uninvited stress (yes, we believe we invite some stress, just think kids' extracurricular activities, clubs, volunteer opportunities, etc.) can take our focus off of the task at hand. As educators with school buildings and classrooms full of children, we can afford distraction about as much as a brain surgeon performing surgery—in other words, we can't. It's important to acknowledge the things that are taking up space in our thoughts and then find appropriate outlets for processing those thoughts and feelings.
5. *Low self-esteem:* Wounds can chip away at our sense of self, purpose, and confidence. As educators, we have young minds seeking their own sense of worth, so we need to be able to recognize our own as we attempt to cultivate self-esteem in others. Greenberg states, "Traumas can destroy self-esteem either because of the injury they cause, or because survivors may feel they did something wrong to deserve such victimization" (2013).
6. *Hypervigilance:* Within the context of traumatic experiences, hypervigilance is like being in a constant state of

"high alert." Being vigilant is a necessity with children in our care, but hypervigilance is not practical or beneficial to our mental well-being or working relationships. Hypervigilance breeds feelings of anxiety and can hinder our ability to respond to situations that do arise with a level head. If we are constantly on guard for negative or threatening outcomes, even an interaction involving a well-intended, constructive criticism might be perceived as a personal attack, and it can feel like we must be ready to combat a crisis at every turn.

7. *Compromised mental and physical health:* We've listed some specifics above, but indeed, unresolved trauma and ongoing adverse experiences can compromise our overall mental and physical health. Compromised mental health is often discussed as a repercussion of trauma in the form of anxiety or depression, but according to research, compromised physical health is also a very real possibility. In an article for Harvard Health Publishing, Dr. Kerry Ressler, a psychiatry professor at Harvard Medical School, states, "Early childhood trauma is a risk factor for almost everything, from adult depression to PTSD and most psychiatric disorders, as well as a host of medical problems, including cardiovascular problems such as heart attack and stroke, cancer, and obesity" (2019).

As you can see, whether from preexisting wounds or current wounds/life stressors, the repercussions to traumatic life events overlap into our workplace. This observation is not a condemnation; rather, it is a reality we need to be sensitive to and honest with ourselves about so that we don't find ourselves experiencing the following repercussions within our work:

1. *Compassion fatigue:* As discussed in Chapter 1, compassion fatigue is a very real job hazard for educators and others constantly exposed to secondary trauma. It stands

to reason that one would be even more susceptible to experiencing compassion fatigue if they still struggle with preexisting trauma and/or ongoing life stress while trying to be a safe harbor for children who need to find a hope and healing in their own lives.

2. *Lowered job performance:* Educators are not alone in this. Just recently, multiple high profile, professional athletes have come forward to share that their compromised mental health has taken a toll on their ability to play their game, which also happens to be their job. At first glance, a professional athlete is the picture of health, but this should be a wakeup call to everyone. Mental health is every bit as important as one's physical health, but it's not always visible on the surface. We are all human, so if we do not tend to ourselves, eventually our ability to tend to the tasks in our workplace will suffer.
3. *Lowered confidence:* When we feel like we aren't putting forth our best efforts, it's easy to feel like we're disappointing ourselves and others, which leads to a lowered sense of confidence. In this line of work, we need to convey a sense of confidence; children tend to have a keen sense of discernment with people, and many times, their own security and confidence ebbs and flows with that of the adults surrounding them.
4. *Dissatisfaction:* There are certainly a multitude of extenuating circumstances that educators blame for job dissatisfaction that include, but are not limited to, standardized testing and not feeling supported. However, carrying the burden of unresolved traumas won't help educators to face the challenges in education today or to experience feelings of satisfaction in the day-to-day investment into the lives of children.
5. *Distrust:* This is a big one. We are going to dive into professional self-care later in the book, but we can tell you this: We cite people over and over throughout these

pages who profess that relationships are key to our well-being. However, some of us have had to contend with wounds that have given us a detrimental outlook on the motives of other people, which results in a lack of trust. Without trust in the workplace, it's hard to keep putting forth effort and find joy in our work.

6. *Burnout:* As mentioned in the first chapter, this is the extreme, but it happens. Again, we are human, and if we don't pay attention to all of the intricacies of ourselves, our experiences (both good and adverse), our interactions, and our beliefs about this world we live in, we could find ourselves overwhelmed to the point of being burnt out.

This was our second summer opening the pool. Unfortunately, after the winter the pool had become green again, but it wasn't as bad as the year before. As we examined the situation this year, it felt more doable and we felt better equipped for how to address the yuck. This time instead of taking months to be resolved, we were able to see a cleared pool in a much shorter amount of time. Our pool is becoming more resilient to the changing seasons as we continue learning how to better care for it with intention.

Like the green of the pool, the repercussions of wounds can resurface after different seasons or experiences, but when we acknowledge them and know how to filter them, we can typically get them balanced a little quicker or call upon someone who helped us do it before. We can become better equipped to accept our wounds as part of our story rather than feel blindsided and rendered helpless or numb by them.

We don't believe any one of you got into education to be devoid of emotion about your jobs or the kids that come through those doorways every day. It's okay to feel sorrow and frustration over the injustices we see. Actually, it's not just okay, it's necessary so that we can also feel empathy for each person, each story that we become intertwined with. If we can find peace somewhere within the complexities of our own stories, we believe we can find hope and empowerment to continue stepping into the stories of those around us and overcome the "green" of the repercussions of our wounds.

Reading, Reflection, and Discussion Points

1. Do you feel like you have experienced any type of desensitization where the word "trauma" is concerned? If so, how might viewing a person as "wounded" give you a new lens for viewing the impact of trauma on children and adults alike?
2. Does knowing that seventy percent of adults have experienced at least one traumatic event make you view the adults in your midst a little bit differently?
3. Do you feel like you've held a judgment card toward yourself or others in how you/they have handled adversity?

   Guidance for book studies and group discussions: The following questions are not meant to put group participants in an awkward position of "full disclosure." Participants should feel free to speak in generalities to prompt healthy, constructive conversation, only sharing personal information and experiences if they feel comfortable doing so. These questions are not meant to create a scenario where participants become counselors for one another; rather, the questions should be used as a springboard to conversation that creates greater sensitivity and insight to the impact of adverse experiences on self and others.
4. Do the typologies of wounds resonate with you personally, as an educator, and/or as a colleague/friend?
5. As mentioned within the chapter, please take a moment to consider the questions about the cycle of wounds and how they impact you, your students, and/or your colleagues or friends:

   - What is my false belief?
   - What does my emotional upheaval look like?

- What are my dysfunctional behaviors (remember, it's not about guilt, it's about vision)?
- What are the resulting life situations (actual or potential)?

6. When considering the Manifestation of Educator Wounds, have you seen any of the repercussions as a challenge with yourself or possibly with colleagues?
7. How might identifying the three most challenging repercussions within your workplace make a difference in the overall culture? Do you think by acknowledging the most challenging personal repercussions for the whole team might be beneficial in combatting their detrimental effects within the workplace (compassion fatigue, lowered job performance, lowered confidence, dissatisfaction, distrust, burnout)?
8. If you or others in your organization are already experiencing some of the six repercussions in the workplace, how is it affecting the overall culture?
9. As you revisit your vision and hope for yourself, how might you add to or adjust it after reading this chapter? How about for your professional setting?

References

Brenner, G. (2017). 6 Ways That a Rough Childhood Can Affect Adult Relationships. Retrieved May 2019, from https://www.psychologytoday.com/us/blog/experimentations/201707/6-ways-rough-childhood-can-affect-adult-relationships

Brown, C. B. (2010). *The gifts of imperfection: Let go of who you think you're supposed to be and embrace who you are.* Center City, MN: Hazelden.

Goulston, M. (2008). *Post-traumatic stress disorder for dummies.* Hoboken, NJ: Wiley Publishing.

Greenberg, M. (2013). Turning to the positive: Personal growth after trauma. Retrieved May 2019, from https://www.psychologytoday.com/us/blog/the-mindful-self-express/201303/turning-the-positive-personal-growth-after-trauma

Harvard Health Publishing. (2019). Past trauma may haunt your future health. Retrieved May 2019, from www.health.harvard.edu/diseases-and-conditions/past-trauma-may-haunt-your-future-health

Marano, N. E. (2003). Our brain's negative bias: Why our brains are more highly attuned to negative news. Retrieved May 2019, from https://www.psychologytoday.com/us/articles/200306/our-brains-negative-bias

Merriam-Webster Online Dictionary. (n.d.). Retrieved August 2019, from https://www.merriam-webster.com/dictionary/cynical

Merriam-Webster Online Dictionary. (n.d.). Retrieved August 2019, from https://www.merriam-webster.com/dictionary/trauma

Perry, B. D., & Szalavitz, M. (2008). *The boy who was raised as a dog: And other stories from a child psychiatrist's notebook: What traumatized children can teach us about loss, love, and healing*. New York, NY: Basic Books.

Sidran Institute. (n.d.). Post Traumatic Stress Disorder Fact Sheet. Retrieved May 2019, from https://www.sidran.org/resources/for-survivors-and-loved-ones/post-traumatic-stress-disorder-fact-sheet/

Van der Kolk, B. A. (2014). *The body keeps the score: Brain, mind, and body in the healing of trauma.* New York, NY: Viking.

Wardle, T. (2007). *Strong winds and crashing waves.* Abilene, TX: Leafwood Publishers.

Pause

We figure half-time or intermission is appropriate at this point. It wasn't easy to revisit our own personal hurdles while writing those first two chapters, so we realize it may have been intense reading them and reflecting on your own personal story, as well. However, we also hope you feel a sense of validation. As educators, we endure an exorbitant amount of pressure and carry a tremendous amount of responsibility. Yet, we are also people with a life outside our calling that presents its own set of challenges, so the whole scenario can feel like we are spinning a lot of plates.

At this juncture, we'd like to reiterate that the intention of this book is to understand the potential effects of secondary trauma, to acknowledge the effects of one's own personal trauma as well as the obstacle it might be creating to effective self-care, and to help launch a healthy vision for change as we move into some doable personal and professional self-care strategies. It is not meant to be a replacement for professional medical assessment and intervention, when necessary. Our desire for this book is to begin healthy conversations, to help people know they aren't alone in the hard of life, and to provide some encouragement and empowerment, too. Anymore, professional therapeutic resources tend to be much more readily available, so please, please utilize them if you need them. We would be remiss in not saying that every person, including you, deserves and are worth it!

Now, if you've had some time to reflect and process a bit and feel ready to forge ahead, let's get started…

3

Creating a Vision for Change

By nature, educators are in the business of identifying cognitive and behavioral concerns with others, namely students, and implementing interventions or strategies to assist them in any perceived areas of weakness. They evaluate the big picture taking into consideration past, present, and future. Many times, plans are put into place to ensure a vision is established to achieve the desired outcome over a period of time.

The desire for self-care strategies involves a need for change because there's a concern for our overall well-being. Status quo is not enough; we want to feel whole, strong, healthy, and enthusiastic about life, both personally and professionally. If we are looking to implement strategies to this end, we believe it's important to create a vision for our own desired outcome. Helen Keller once said, "The only thing worse than being blind is having sight but no vision."

The best way we have found for clarifying one's vision is to start by identifying the areas of concern by asking the following questions:

- Why are we trying to make change?
- What are we seeking to change?
- Who are we trying to change?

Why Are We Trying to Make Change?

We've already discussed that the rigors of being in education are taking their toll on professionals emotionally and physically. People are becoming dissatisfied in their chosen profession, and this is not good news for the professional educator or those around them, so the reasons are numerous for understanding compassion fatigue, woundedness, and then getting intentional with self-care:

- *Educators are physically and emotionally tired*. Think about it, as educators, we must make hundreds (maybe more!) of decisions every day, and many of those decisions must be made on the fly. This requires a huge amount of mental energy and focus. Add to that the emotional investment we make into our students day after day. It is necessary for us to tap into a multitude of skill sets, and sometimes we are even required to make up new skill sets because the needs of our students are ever evolving. We strive to create environments conducive to learning while exercising restraint in the face of children's behavioral challenges, a disgruntled parent, or frustrations within the workplace. The emotional toll rolls into a physical toll, yet any profession where children are involved requires nothing less than operating on all cylinders. Not being able to do so can contribute to a higher rate of absenteeism, which in turn can create even higher levels of stress within a profession that thrives on structure and consistency.

- *Educators want to make an impact.* In order to impact our student population for the better, we need to be at peak performance. If we are constantly operating from a place of depletion, our performance and even our ability to complete tasks is jeopardized. Not only that, when we feel we are not working to our potential or making a significant contribution through our profession, it feels like a major blow to our sense of purpose and satisfaction in our work.
- *Educators need balance.* Our commitment to our students runs deep. So deep, in fact, that we can easily be devoting mental and physical energy to our students well past the final bell of each day. Whether we are carrying the burdens of our students home with us or devising new methods to enhance their education, if we aren't careful, our jobs can impede our personal lives. There's no such thing as caring too much (we'll discuss this more later), but it's imperative for us to be able to make space for our families, our friendships, our hobbies, and ourselves.
- *Educators need an emotionally safe workplace.* Think about it; if we're all walking around out of balance and operating from a place of depletion, feeling like our work is subpar to boot, our tendency toward a short fuse is exacerbated. Working within an educational organization requires much patience, communication, and collaboration, but if we find ourselves overwhelmed, we can easily contribute to a "walking on eggshells" culture. In reality, what we need is to feel the same emotional safety our students crave so that we feel supported, encouraged, and like we have a place to be authentic about our challenges with the expectation that our teammates will come alongside us. This sense of emotional safety contributes to the overall morale of your building. Just as our students need to feel safe to learn, educators need to feel safe to create, contribute, and thrive.

- *Educators need to feel empowered to evolve.* Many people resist change not necessarily because they are stubborn, but because change involves a lot of mental energy. Change can also be difficult to navigate if you already feel exhausted or if you feel alone in trying to tackle it. However, change is inevitable, especially when trying to keep pace with the everchanging demands in the field of education. It's a whole lot easier to embrace (or at least not resist) change if we're not constantly feeling like we are about to buckle under the pressures of life.
- *Emotional investment is required of educators.* Kids have an uncanny ability to sense whether a person is checked in or checked out emotionally with them, and if they feel like you're checked out, chances are, they will check out, too. This is not an ideal scenario when our goal is to connect with our students on a relational level that encourages learning. Emotional investment can be hard for a lot of reasons. We might feel drained, we might have other things going on in our lives outside the classroom, a kid might push our buttons so hard that we want to put up a wall, or it just might feel scary because that emotional investment can lead to heartache. Whatever the obstacle might be, the reality remains the same: People need people not just to show up, but to pour out, and there's no truer example of this than looking at the needs of a child. Their relationships with the significant adults in their lives will have a lasting influence on the relationships they cultivate in their futures, and in this life, we need real, invested connections with one another, spurring us on to become the very best version of ourselves.
- *This world needs educators.* We are going to speak as parents of children who have experienced trauma on this one. We need educators. We need you to teach our children. We need you to love and encourage our children.

We need your presence and investment to continue shining light into the dark places where false beliefs might have a stronghold on our babies. Your voice and influence carry a lot of weight in the lives of our children because they don't always believe Mom and Dad when we say they are strong, they are smart, and that they matter. We cannot continue to lose good educators. You are an integral part of our family's team, and so selfishly, we want you to feel whole and able to continue doing what you do so beautifully. You may not always see it in the mundane, but in the big picture, you matter a great deal to our children, to our communities, and to the future.

What Are We Seeking to Change?

The "why's" listed above are quite compelling, and you might even have a few to add to the list depending on your particular situation. In any case, identifying the "why" can assist us in moving on to examining the "what." What we'd like to change about our dilemma with compassion fatigue and self-care can be a multitude of things, but here are several that we've heard consistently from practitioners on the front line:

- *Educators want to be heard.* Educators want to influence educational policies and procedures through the lens of a practitioner. It's frustrating to have someone tell you how to conduct business in your schools and classrooms when they've never experienced the reality of what that looks like or entails.
- *Educators want social justice.* There's a huge discrepancy in funding for schools, and many times educators dig into their own pockets to provide adequate resources and opportunities for their students' learning. It becomes disheartening when you feel like "your kids"

aren't getting a fair shake. It is also overwhelming when the burden of creating an equal playing field for preparing "your kids" to measure up to all the same academic criteria as students in other schools with greater resources falls on you.

- *Educators want social emotional support for students.* The latest statistics find that 47.9 percent of children have experienced at least one traumatic experience. Educators can play a huge role in positioning children to experience hope and transformation in their lives through education, but many times children and their families need access to additional supports to meet their emotional and physical needs. Additionally, most everyone we've spoken with wishes their guidance counselors weren't so encumbered by testing and scheduling so they could be available for additional support with students who need it.
- *Educators want smaller class sizes.* Beyond some of the evidence-based reasons for reducing class sizes to increase academic achievement, educators often state they would choose smaller class sizes to be able to offer more individualized attention to students and be able to create a stronger sense of community.
- *Educators want to feel supported by their leadership and communities.* Somewhere along the line, there's become a disconnect within our schools between teachers and administrators. This is sticky for Joe because he's been on both sides of the coin, and there are certainly times we observed a culture that became an "us versus them" attitude instead of the collaboration education should be and needs to be. This disconnect affects morale where people feel isolated and the overall culture can feel divisive and even toxic. Depending on the year and circumstances, educators can also long for better parental support and involvement, and they long for

society to be a source of encouragement instead of ridicule. The very nature of school funding in some states can give educators the impression that they aren't supported when levies aren't passed and criticism for educators' schedules and salaries becomes a point of contention.

- *Educators want autonomy.* We probably don't need to say much more than that, but we will. We each have unique styles and skill sets, not to mention we continue to hone our craft through ongoing professional learning opportunities. We want others to assume competence and allow us to deliver the content we have to share not geared toward achievement on a standardized test, but in a way that is uniquely ours which encourages young minds to be curious, seek more information, and ultimately, retain that information to use within the context of life. We also have the desire to be able to gauge achievement with a measuring stick that doesn't expect everyone to learn the same way and that takes into consideration the complex variables involved with each child's life and learning.

This is probably a mere scratching of the surface for the "what" we'd like to change in order for us to not risk experiencing so much stress and compassion fatigue in our profession, but these cover some of the top frustrations we've heard across the country. Let us now ask you a hard question: Do you have any direct control over any of these issues? If you happen to be in a position to right the ship in any of these areas, by all means, do so. But for most people in education, these areas of concern and frustration are not anything we can change just because we want to or think we have a better answer. This reality probably lends itself to even further feelings of stress because let's face it, we'd feel more comfortable if we felt like we had some control in these matters. Let's see about finding some relief in the next question.

Who Are We Trying to Change?

It's probably not terribly difficult to begin a running list of "who" in your head. After all, we are educators and as mentioned earlier, it's our job on a daily basis to sum up concerns we have with students, so that easily translates to the people around us. Your "who" might include:

- *Students:* It becomes very frustrating when students seem unmotivated, distracted, or that they just don't give a rip about doing their work. Others may exhibit attitudes and/or behaviors that try our patience on an epic level. Yet others might have a heartbreaking sadness about them that penetrates your own heart to the point of agonizing discomfort.
- *Parents:* We wish every parent would be supportive of their children as well as those educating them instead of just pockets of support varying from year to year. We wish parents would make sure their kiddos are well fed, rested, and that they've been taught appropriate boundaries and respect for others. We want them to read with their children, provide accountability with their children, and not take offense to any constructive criticisms or suggestions we might offer to help their child be more successful in school.
- *My boss/administration:* Some people love their leadership and others not so much. The biggest complaints we hear are that the administration isn't supportive or encouraging, they blame us for low test scores, they don't step into tough behavioral situations when we need them, they allow negative employees to run the show, they don't treat us like we are valued or appreciated, they only care about the data, they (you may have more concerns to fill in the blank).

- *My staff:* Educational administrators can face their own adversities in the leadership role. As Joe removes the teacher hat and replaces it with his former school administrator cap, he can speak to a few things: They might wish their staff trusted them, that they understood some decisions are made based on the information known only by the administrator in the heat of the moment, that some people got into administration not to exercise their power, but to feel like they could help make a greater impact in the lives of children, that sometimes bureaucracy leaves their hands tied, that sometimes their hearts are broken, too.
- *My coworkers:* We hear time and again that people feel so defeated by the attitudes of their coworkers. Some feel trapped in an unhealthy culture where too many team members don't appear to care. Others feel frustrated with clashing philosophies and the inability to have constructive conversations without them becoming personal. Still others feel isolated within their professional community.
- *My school board:* Many educators feel handcuffed at times by their school boards, and the biggest complaint is that the board is typically comprised of people who are not trained in education, yet they are making critical decisions involving the educational system all the time.
- *All the people that say educators are overpaid:* It's hard and exhausting to feel like you must defend your chosen profession at every turn and justify your paycheck. It's even harder to feel like people don't respect or value what is arguably one of the hardest, most important jobs there is.

There may be other "who's" that come to mind for you, but this covers a good bit of ground. Seeing all the potential "who's" that we'd like to change probably isn't feeling like much relief like we suggested we might find as we left the last section. Do you know why? As an educator, Joe rarely tells people the answer in absolutes because it's an educator's job to allow space for critical thinking and problem solving since it appears about ninety percent of everything falls into grey area. However, on this one, we're going to tell you the answer. There is no relief to be found in identifying any of the above as the "who" because we have absolutely no control over any of them. None. Zero. Nada.

It has taken us many years to realize what a trap it is to think we can control anyone except—and here's where some of the relief comes—we can control ourselves. Here's the thing: We may not be able to control anyone else's attitudes, behaviors, or thinking, but we can be an influence. We can make a difference in the lives of our students. We can contribute to a paradigm shift in our workplaces. We can be an encouragement and empowering presence with the various stakeholders we encounter every day.

Where does it begin? It begins with the acceptance that anything worthwhile typically doesn't happen overnight. It begins with self-definition and practice and intention and perseverance and stumbling and getting back up again. It's being humble and confident about where you've been and where you're headed all at once. It begins with envisioning something better and recognizing the power of your contribution to that end.

One of our favorite quotes has always been, "You must be the change you wish to see in the world" (Mahatma Gandhi). Effecting change is not a one and done. It goes deeper than throwing some change in a bucket or treating the person behind you in the Starbucks drive thru. These are nice in the moment, but to effect long term, lasting change involves a lot of determination and a daily decision to be the change in spite of the world's push-back. And there will be push-back. Why? The short answer is because people become comfortable with what they know, even if they don't like it or feel good about it. However, nothing changes if nothing changes. All of us are free to choose what we do, what we say, and how we respond every day. What we don't get to choose are the consequences to our choices. For instance, the administrator or teacher who throws blame and shame for a rough set of test scores cannot expect the response to be a rise in morale or a boost in confidence. More than likely, a culture of fear and distrust will take root instead. Choosing wisely and thoughtfully doesn't guarantee you'll get back what you put forth, but the odds are in your favor and ultimately, you'll feel better about yourself.

Where does it move forward? It moves forward with investing in ourselves, acknowledging where our own wounds and false beliefs might be creating barriers to hope. It begins with recognizing the importance of and intentionally implementing self-care strategies. It begins with the knowing that nurturing the best version of ourselves will have a ripple effect into every interaction, every task, and every relationship we encounter. It will be hard at first, and it will take time and intention, even some trial and error, but when you create your own safe space to operate from, you can find peace and hope in the adversities of being an educator.

Reading, Reflection, and Discussion Points

1. What is the benefit of bringing definition to your personal and professional vision?
2. Have you ever been intentional with creating a vision for yourself at some point in your career? If so, are you mindful of it within your days or has it become lost?
3. Does your organization have a clear vision with regard to creating a healthy, productive culture?
4. Do you have a "why" from the "Why are we trying to change?" list that resonates with you more than the others?
5. Do you have a "why" not included on the list?
6. Do you have a "what" from the "What are we trying to change?" list that resonates with you more than the others?
7. Do you have a "what" not included on the list?

8. Who would you change if you could and why? That may seem like a loaded question if you read through the whole chapter! It's not a trick question—go ahead and answer honestly.
9. Consider your response to the last question. Knowing that the only "who" you can really change is yourself, how might you influence your organization's culture in the way you wish you could see the change in the "who" you described in the last question?
10. As you revisit your vision and hope for yourself, how might you add to or adjust it after reading this chapter? How about for your professional setting?

References

Helen Keller Quotes. (n.d.). BrainyQuote.com. Retrieved October 2019, from https://www.brainyquote.com/quotes/helen_keller_383771

Mahatma Gandhi Quotes. (n.d.). BrainyQuote.com. Retrieved October 2019, from https://www.brainyquote.com/quotes/mahatma_gandhi_109075

4

Personal Strategies for Self-Care

Do you ever feel like when it comes to self-care, the discussion immediately goes to "eat right, get enough sleep, and exercise"? We don't know about you, but that can feel like an admonishment rather than an encouragement, especially if we happen to be in the middle of a candy bar at three o'clock in the afternoon. Yes, we fall into the category of people who wishes stress would drive us to do household chores instead of reach for simple carbs. Anyway, we totally agree that eating right, exercising, and getting good sleep are great for our overall health, but what happens when stress hijacks our good intentions?

We also see the traits "grit" and "resilience" thrown around a lot these days as the difference between those who "make it" and those who continue struggling through life. Grit is defined as courage and resolve; strength of character, whereas resilience is the capacity to recover quickly from difficulties; toughness (online dictionary, n.d.). Grit and resilience are great in the right context, but they sure can come across in the wrong context as "pull yourself up by the bootstraps." This adage is neither helpful nor appropriate in the face of an educator who is limping along. Grit and resilience should be seen as healthy by-products of self-care and not character flaws or signs of weakness if they are temporarily compromised.

We also believe that self-care goes beyond retail therapy and bubble baths. While these kinds of things provide a temporary respite from stress, the stress is still there once the water goes cold or the card is maxed out, which becomes its own kind of stress! We'd like to suggest that good self-care should position us to handle the inevitable stresses of life, which in turn compliments pursuing a healthy lifestyle, increasing our capacity for grit and resilience, and allowing us to be fully present to enjoy the fun moments of life, whether that entails making memories with people we care about or a bubble bath!

Sound easy? To be honest, it's not. What we have learned through numerous difficult seasons is that there's no quick fix to disappointment, hurt, fatigue (emotional and/or physical), fear, doubt, turmoil, bitterness, (fill in the blank). We have found that it takes commitment and intentional effort with arguably the most significant relationship you have: The relationship with yourself. From Dardi's vantage point as the spouse of an educator, now the mother of adult children who are educators, and the parent of children who experienced early trauma that has impacted their interactions in the classroom and at home, she believes she is justified in saying that educators as much as anyone, and maybe even more so, are "up against it" in their chosen profession. Not only do you face the realities of the daily challenges of meeting so many diverse needs in your students, you are up against the perception that teachers are overpaid, the fear of a violent incident in the workplace, and now there's high stakes testing thrown into the mix. In reality, commitment and intentional effort should probably read more like we must fight like hell for our mental well-being. Woodrow Wilson once said, "You are not here merely to make a living. You are here in order to enable the world to live more amply, with greater vision, with a finer spirit of hope and achievement. You are here to enrich the world, and you impoverish yourself if you forget the errand."

Before we go any further, we would like to preface these suggestions for self-care with a statement mentioned previously in the book that Joe makes often when he's out speaking and teaching: It's not about guilt, it's about vision, which we hope at this point in the book you are beginning to feel empowered by as you reflect on a vision for yourself. The suggestions we are putting forth are not grounded in us having life all figured out and just waiting for everyone else to get with the program. More often than not, these strategies were born out of all the ways we army crawled through the muck of life when we could have opted for a less messy, less arduous route. Our point is we are all on a journey, and these are some of the things we have found to be extremely helpful in navigating life's craziness through a lens of vision and hope.

Self-Care Strategy #1: Journal

If you saw "journal" and your eyes glazed over, you're not the first person to respond this way, but hang in there with us. We completely understand if your first thought is, "That sounds like work, and I don't have time for one more thing." We get it, we really do, but check this out: According to the American Psychological Association (2001),

> Writing about stressful events has long been known to cause improvements in health and psychological well-being. Now, a new study provides clues to why that is. The research, published in the September issue of APA's *Journal of Experimental Psychology: General (JEP: General)* (Vol. 130, No. 3), indicates that expressive writing reduces intrusive and avoidant thoughts about negative events and improves working memory. These improvements,

> researchers believe, may in turn free up our cognitive resources for other mental activities, including our ability to cope more effectively with stress.

Simply put, journaling is a safe place to decompress negative emotions and situations. However, we also think it's important to write about your personal aspirations as well as noteworthy positive feelings and interactions. According to author Atlas Rowe (n.d.),

> …having a goal can actually help make you happier. Seriously, it can. You see, people who have written down their goals, and commit to go after something bigger and better than what they have today, creates hope. Hope for a better tomorrow, hope for a better future, hope that the happiness they seek can actually be achieved.

There are no specific rules to follow regarding your journal, but we suggest that the goal for your journal would be to become a space where hope is realized amid chaos and stress. Lest you have some picture in your head of one of us writing in our journal in a field of wildflowers with the sun shining down while a gentle breeze is blowing, we'll clue you into the reality. Dardi has been journaling for about fourteen years now, and sometimes she has to lock herself in our room and hide behind the bed to make it happen. Joe hasn't been journaling for as long, but sometimes it's a little easier for him just because he travels. Hint: If you don't live alone or at least among self-sufficient humans, don't try hiding in the bathroom; it never works. People with children of the human or four-legged variety will understand this directive without further explanation.

There have been times where we have written in our journals almost daily, and then suddenly, weeks have passed where we haven't opened their pages. Typically, we each come to the realization that we've neglected our journaling because we either feel overwhelmed, excessively cranky, or a combination thereof. We don't give ourselves a guilt trip about it, but we will carve out some time (stat!) to do a little regrouping within our respective journals. Again, make your journal *yours*. If you are feeling a little stuck or overwhelmed about where to start, here are a few suggestions (we do not use all of these ourselves, but different things appeal to different folks):

- Lament feelings about tough situations or interactions
- Brainstorm solutions
- Set goals
- Practice gratitude
- Acknowledge emotional triggers
- Celebrate victories
- Collect nuggets of wisdom and inspiration
- Keep notes from a daily devotional
- Hopes and prayers for self and others

The list can easily go on, but you get the idea. Marinella (2017) shares, "Journal writing gives us insights into who we are, who we were, and who we can become." Again, the point is to create a safe space that is uniquely yours where you can unload your burdens, be authentic and vulnerable with your feelings, and free up space in your mind to focus on the beautiful moments and possibilities in your life.

Self-Care Strategy #2: Choose Your Words Wisely

We're pretty sure you've all heard, "If you don't have anything nice to say, don't say anything at all." We've found that to be pretty solid advice in the context of relationships with others, but have you considered it as it pertains to the relationship with yourself? The words we speak to ourselves (whether verbally or by thought) hold so much power, so much so that our very words can become the obstacles to hope and healthy self-definition.

According to Dr. Gregory L. Jantz, "Each of us has a set of messages that play over and over in our minds. This internal dialogue, or personal commentary, frames our reactions to life and its circumstances. One of the ways to recognize, promote, and sustain optimism, hope, and joy is to intentionally fill our thoughts with positive self-talk" (2016).

So where does all this negative self-talk come from? Dr. Jantz goes on to say, "Too often, the pattern of self-talk we've developed is negative. We remember the negative things we were told as children by our parents, siblings, or teachers. We remember the negative reactions from other children that diminished how we felt about ourselves. Throughout the years, these messages have played over and over in our minds, fueling our feelings of anger, fear, guilt, and hopelessness" (2016).

Being intentional with positive self-talk is not an effort to diminish or negate hurtful experiences or to gloss over any of our less than stellar moments. Rather, it's an empowerment tool for embedding truth into lies and false beliefs that harshly try to define us and maybe even cripple us in our work and relationships, at times. A few years back, we did an experiential exercise during one of our Wounded Educator sessions. It involved listing negative experiences on an index card that might be adversely impacting participants' thought processes toward themselves and then replacing it with an "I am ____________" statement based in truth on a separate paper they could keep with them. They were invited to place their "adversity card" in a basket on the way out as a symbolic way of laying down the heavy load they might be carrying. We weren't really sure how this would play out in such a short conference breakout session, but the majority of people placed their adversity cards in the basket. We specifically asked that no one share any identifying information on the cards for privacy, so we spent some time going through the cards to get an idea about the battles people were fighting against in their minds. We were humbled and heartbroken over the transparency shared on those index cards about self-image issues, anxiety, depression, feelings of failure or inadequacy, childhood abuse, divorce, to name a few, that led people to feelings of shame, self-doubt, and negativity. We will never forget one card in particular where a man wrote down that he had been a victim of abuse when he was a little boy, and for a long time, his defining words were, "I am a victim, weak, ashamed." He shared his new "I am" statement, and it looked like this: "I AM A SURVIVOR." Such a powerful truth that doesn't for one second discount what he'd been through, but instead says, "In spite of…." Two completely different statements: One broken and defeated, the other full of strength, hope, and truth.

Even beyond healthy self-definition are very real health benefits derived from positive self-talk. According to one article,

> Positive self-talk is a direct spin-off of positive emotions. It is the physical manifestation of your psyche encouraging you, and it's proven to have numerous benefits. Unfortunately, research shows that 80% of an average person's thoughts in one day are negative and self-deprecating. Only 20% of our inner dialogue even remotely resembles positive thought, and it's high time we changed that.
>
> Good Relaxation, 2016

The article goes on to say that the top three benefits of positive self-talk are:

1. Stress reduction
2. Confidence booster
3. Better relationships (Good Relaxation, 2016)

These look like some awesome benefits for everyone, especially educators! Positive self-talk takes lots of practice and loads of intention. Tugaleva suggests, "When you love people, you are curious about who they are, what they think, and how they feel. You watch them closely, wondering about their experience and what you can do to make it more enjoyable. You feel compassion for their pain and seek to make it more bearable. You are eager to learn the unique language of their existence. You want to understand them, inspire them, heal them. What if you could look at yourself this way?" (2017). For whatever reason, the human tendency seems to find criticizing self to be almost effortless, so we would propose that this is where journaling would also be beneficial in reinforcing positivity and empowerment toward self.

Personal Self-Care Strategy #3: Know Your Triggers

What is not fun is being accosted by overwhelming feelings that you are unprepared for, and as mentioned earlier in the book, there's nothing like a child in the midst of their own behavior or response rooted in trauma to bring out our own triggers. Unfortunately, we can also be triggered by just about anyone or anything within the scope of our day, be it verbal or situational. There are certainly emotional triggers that bring about those warm fuzzy, nostalgic feelings, but that's not what we're discussing here. We're talking about moments that take us back to a negative encounter we've had that's threatened our sense of security and well-being. Regarding emotional triggers, Davies states, "Most of us will undergo negative experiences in our life, and emotional triggers stem from these. They are sudden and painful reminders of a negative incident in the past that stirs up powerful emotions. They come to the surface when you are faced with a similar position and if not dealt with can overwhelm and control you" (n.d.).

What does a negative emotional trigger look like? First, it will be different for everyone based on personal experiences. If we go back to Dr. Wardle's typology of wounds, it can be helpful in identifying life experiences that may be at the root of our personal triggers. As Joe has shared, the situation with taking a gun away from his dad has had an impact on his reactions to other life situations. If he perceives something to be life threatening in any way, he can easily be triggered into feelings of anxiety and helplessness. My emotional triggers are different. Having been in an abusive relationship as a young adult, I've learned to recognize that it is easy for me to feel controlled or disrespected in response to anything perceived as hostility or dishonesty. The responses to emotional triggers are as varied as the triggers themselves, but some typical responses include:

- You feel overcome by fear.
- You feel an overwhelming grief or sadness.
- You feel anxiety.
- You become defensive.
- You feel threatened or personally attacked.
- You feel harassed (emotionally or physically).
- You feel shame or unworthiness.
- You experience feelings of helplessness.
- You feel anger.
- You feel excluded or not valued.
- You experience feelings of injustice.

Having emotional triggers does not make us weak; it makes us human. What makes us feel weak is being caught off guard by our triggers and allowing the ensuing emotions and responses to take over our functioning. Finding ourselves in emotional disarray does not bode well given that our clientele (children and adolescents) thrive on emotional consistency, especially if they have known chaos and trauma in their lives. Instead, we benefit our mental well-being by identifying our triggers and then having a practiced response so they don't suddenly have control over our emotional steering wheel. Practiced responses to triggers are like pouring truth into false beliefs. Some practiced responses might include:

- *"This isn't personal. They don't know my history enough to use it against me."*

- *"I am the tangible presence that represents the reality behind that child's anger."*
- *"I am equipped and capable to handle this situation."*
- *"Their behavior is a reflection of their own struggle, it has nothing to do with me."*
- *"I recognize these feelings and where they are coming from, but I have the final say in how I feel and respond in this moment."*

These are a few examples, but you get the idea. Empower yourself to define your responses, to categorize your feelings, and to draw strength from knowing that you are more than able to boss your triggers into submission. As it pertains to self-care, this is one of the best things you can do for yourself as well as those around you because you will feel a sense of peace and control instead of constantly being tossed around by chaos and at the mercy of what might be around the corner.

Self-Care Strategy #4: Unplug

Many years ago, we lived next door to Dardi's grandparents. Being the practical people they were (not to mention the fact we were a young family living on a teacher's salary), Grandpa would daily deliver his copy of the newspaper to our mail slot after he had finished reading it. We loved taking a break from all the usual things for a half hour or so to read the latest local and world happenings. The biggest controversy you'd find in those pages was who made the traffic log or the "In the Courts" section. Occasionally, someone was brave enough to put their name to a "Letter to the Editor" (no anonymous submissions were allowed) with their opinion of a perceived local, national, or world atrocity, and the closest thing to anything foodie or Pinterest worthy was the Thursday spotlight on someone in the community sharing their favorite family recipes. Political news stuck to pretty much the facts without any added opinions or extensive analyzing, and the sports were just the game recaps with stats minus most of the fanfare and drama we've come to expect. Sounds almost archaic, right? (The newspaper situation, not us!)

Fast forward a few trips around the sun, and we have up to the minute news on anything and everything literally at our fingertips. Let's be real. In today's world, the thought of unplugging is not only hard, but probably unpopular at first consideration. Having immediate access to people and information is fantastic if we're researching something important, especially when recollecting our tedious childhood go-to of an outdated set of encyclopedias. We can communicate, book travel reservations, check out recipes, shop, do our banking, and accomplish a multitude of other mundane tasks from the comfort of the couch. However, studies (and personal experience) are suggesting we spend a whole lot of time checking out by logging in. According to Mary Meeker's 2018 Internet Trends study (Molla, 2018), the average adult user in 2017 spent 5.9 hours with digital media. The Nielsen Total Audience Report from the first quarter of 2018 states that overall total media use among U.S. adults is at eleven hours per day. We could probably continue to find stats all day long, and we did look at others, but the overall theme is we are spending an excessive amount of time staring at screens and not leaving much time for anything else. Granted, some of that time involves our occupations, but what about our personal time? What difference does the amount of time we spend online make regarding self-care? Let's consider a few things:

1. *Anxiety/stress:* Gone are the days of Grandpa dropping off the newspaper, so we admit it, our information highway tends to be social media. We can always depend on certain friends to keep us abreast with links to the very latest news articles. The flaw in this avenue is that we end up scrolling through a bunch of stuff we don't need to know, we don't want to know, and inevitably, there's that one comment that makes the eye get a twitch (we know,

don't read the comments). More often than not, what once upon a time was a half hour check-in on the world and brief escape from the mundane of the day turns into a much longer encounter that ends with having to convince ourselves to back away from the keyboard before joining in on some controversial drama. Instead of feeling like we just took a break, we're now reciting arguments in our brains and taking on battles we can't win. This is not refreshing or good for stress levels!

2. *Feelings of discontent:* Along with the anxiety and stress social media can create, the worldwide web as a whole breeds feelings of discontent. No matter if you're looking for specific information or mindlessly scrolling, you're bound to see one image after another that could make you feel like crap about your life. Holden advises, "Beware of destination addiction—a preoccupation with the idea that happiness is in the next place, the next job, and with the next partner. Until you give up the idea that happiness is somewhere else, it will never be where you are" (2011). The bottom line is that advertisements are meant to make you feel like you're missing out on something you really must have to make your life complete, and the majority of personal stuff you see on social media is a highlight reel. The reality is, it's not reality, but the constant exposure to it lures us into feelings of discontent.
3. *Missed opportunities for authentic interactions:* People, we need each other. We need real, authentic relationships and friendships. Dardi tends to be more of an extrovert, while Joe leans more toward being an introvert, but as human beings, we both still need people. We love what Dr. Bruce Perry says:

> For years, mental health professionals taught people that they could be psychologically healthy without social support, that "unless you love

> yourself, no one else will love you" … The truth is, you cannot love yourself unless you have been loved and are loved. The capacity to love cannot be built in isolation.
>
> Perry & Szalavitz, 2008

The digital age has created such a false sense of connection with others. Don't get us wrong; technology has bridged many a gap to make long distance communication not only possible, but immediate. This is so amazing when being face to face isn't an option. Four of our adult children live far enough away that we can't just stop by, so we love our family text messages where we can touch base with all the updates and funnies of life. But when one of them shows up for a surprise visit or calls to talk? No text, no e-mail, no social media post in the world measures up. When we are tuned into our devices, though, we are tuned out of life. We miss the opportunity to engage with our most treasured people, to catch up with a neighbor, to enjoy a brief chat with a stranger, or to just plain experience the authenticity that comes through eye contact and hearing the emotion behind someone's words.

4. *You can't "unsee" some things:* You're an educator, so chances are you've seen some things along your professional journey that you wish you hadn't, but that's become an occupational hazard of being in education. I'm not suggesting we bury our heads in the sand, but we can choose to limit our exposure to the barrage of negativity and graphic nature of the readily available content online. The emotional demands put in front of you every day are significant enough; you don't need to subject yourself to more things that feel too heavy for your heart and mind to bear.
5. *Avoidance:* This is a tough one, so let's rip off the proverbial band-aid… We need to learn to be okay being alone

with ourselves. This shouldn't be confused with isolation, but every one of us needs some undisturbed time to process through our thoughts, our encounters, and our emotions, some of which are hard and uncomfortable. Concerning emotional avoidance, Dr. Noam Shpancer (2010) states, "Over time, avoidance becomes a prison, because after a while you begin to feel the need to avoid many situations, people, experiences and places that may bring the negative emotion to mind, stir it, or remind you of it. And the more you avoid, the weaker you feel, the more your coping skills diminish, and the less of life you can experience." When we are constantly occupying our minds with other people, other places, and other things via the worldwide web, we are creating a neglected cesspool of emotions. As foster parents, we encountered several children who were medicated for their emotional upheaval. We are not at all anti-medication; it can be a very useful tool when used appropriately, but the problem we saw with these particular kiddos was that the medication temporarily masked their inner turmoil, but as the medication wore off, the grief, anger, and fear were still there and ready to spill over with a vengeance. As human beings, we are meant to experience our emotions, the good ones and the hard ones, but we have to be careful to avoid self-medicating through the Internet or some other form of avoidance because we're only setting ourselves up to feel stuck and anxious. We will again mention that this is where keeping a journal can be helpful, but we also want to encourage you that if you find yourself trying to unpack some emotions that are beyond sorting out through some quiet space and/or journaling, please don't hesitate to ask a professional for help in doing so. A healthy, objective lens to assist you in walking through painful or difficult thoughts or feelings could be the very best gift you give yourself.

6. *Overly busy mind:* We also need time to try not to think at all! We're sure you've heard the term "mental break." Our minds need to be able to rest, but rest does not come through scrolling the news, the sports, the latest entertainment scandals, the social media channels, the (you fill in the blank) for all the reasons listed above. Beth Janes states, "Time off is what your brain thrives on. It spends hours every day working and managing the constant streams of information and conversation that come at you from all directions. But if your brain doesn't get a chance to chill and restore itself, your mood, performance, and health suffer. Think of this recovery as mental downtime-periods when you're not actively focusing on and engaged in the outside world. You simply let your mind wander or daydream and it becomes re-energized in the process" (2019). Further, Dr. Stew Friedman says, "The mind needs rest. Research shows that after you take a mental time-out, you are better at creative thinking and coming up with solutions and new ideas, and you feel more content" (2014).
7. *Missing out on mind, heart, & soul stimulation:* If we are filling all our time and space on a device, we've left no room for anything else. It's important to have time to read something for fun or that stimulates our minds and to feed our spiritual side through time in nature or study/prayer/meditation. We already mentioned how time on our devices is jeopardizing the opportunity for authentic connection, but it's worth repeating that we must leave space for relational connections, which we will continue to emphasize as an imperative aspect of overall wellbeing.

Friends, we aren't suggesting you go completely off grid. That would pretty much equate to telling Joe to give up dark chocolate. It's not happening. However, we can make sure that the quantity and quality of time invested in our devices is not turning what could be a harmless encounter into an all-out binge that leaves us in a worse emotional state than when we started and inhibits us from being an active participant in life. Even Steven Spielberg, a man whose professional life is dependent on technology, has said, "Technology can be our best friend, and technology can also be the biggest party pooper of our lives. It interrupts our own story, interrupts our ability to have a thought or a daydream, to imagine something wonderful, because we're too busy bridging the walk from the cafeteria back to the office on the cell phone" (Kennedy, 2002).

Self-Care Strategy #5: Learn to Say No

Dardi learned this strategy from a precious teacher friend of hers a number of years ago. She was on a planning committee for weekday church school and put in charge of recruiting volunteers to teach. Dardi was encouraged to try to recruit school teachers since the dates for the program would be in early June, and teachers would be on summer break by then! Yay! (You can probably already see where this is going, keep reading.) So, she happily set down with her teacher friend and invited her to participate in this most wonderful volunteer opportunity that was most certainly right up her alley, and she told Dardi, "No." That "no" was one of the biggest revelations in her life, though! This teacher proceeded with brutal honesty and said, "Dardi, I love kids, but by the end of the school year, I want, no I NEED, to do something else for a while." Dardi shares, "People, I saw the light. I have nine children, so naturally, others assume anything involving children or adolescents is my thing. I am recruited for every volunteer opportunity child-related. I love children, it is true, but I've also been raising children for most of my adult life, so I, too, want and even need to invest in some other things that involve the grown variety of people occasionally. I also enjoy spending time with animals at the shelter, but that landed us a puppy, so Joe learned to exercise his own no. Anyway…"

It's easy to feel like others are compartmentalizing us bas on what they see and know of us, but we only have to be in that box if we've allowed it. Are there still times we say yes when we really don't feel like it? Of course there are because sometimes the score book needs kept, or the class is going to need cookies (we are very much still in the stage of school-aged activities, but you see our point). However, it is not only okay, but necessary, to create healthy boundaries by declining requests that create anxious, burdensome feelings within. Not only that, if we are constantly filling space with things that are not feeding our souls, chances are we are missing out on participating in opportunities that make our hearts beat. Be sure your yes to other people is not a no to you.

It's also important to learn to say no if you are naturally a people pleaser, or if your tendency is to be involved in everything for fear of not being busy with something. Brown states, "One of the most universal numbing strategies is what I call 'crazy-busy'" (2012). When asked to elaborate on this quote for an article in the *Washington Post*, Brown explains, "'Crazy-busy' is a great armor, it's a great way for numbing. What a lot of us do is that we stay so busy, and so out in front of our life, that the truth of how we're feeling and what we really need can't catch up with us" (Cunningham, 2012). Just like with unplugging, we need to be sure we are allowing ourselves space to relax and just be. Healthy boundaries with work and commitments are just that: Healthy for mind, body, and soul.

Self-Care Strategy #6: Learn to Say Yes

We are very well aware that we just finished suggesting that you learn to say no, and we absolutely stand by that. However, we've found that people who haven't found this balance yet fall into one of two habits: (1) People struggle with exercising their no, so they fill any available time doing things they don't feel passionate about or with anything at all (see above) and don't have any time or energy left to do anything else or (2) People that have already learned to exercise their no may take it to the extreme and say no to pretty much everything. Neither mode is any good or even fun. We really want to encourage you to take a step back and see where you might be missing out. Do you have a personal or professional idea you've been toying with? Say yes. Has someone invited you to do something that maybe takes you a bit out of your comfort zone but also sounds intriguing? Say yes. Does a little person want to paint your nails with sparkly nail polish? Say yes (In our house, Daddy was just recently sporting a beautiful blue glittery polish on his thumbs for a week!).

Or here's one: Has someone offered to do something kind for you? Say yes. Please say yes. Why is this one so hard? We can tell you why. We are prideful people, that's why. And we don't want to be a bother. Maybe it's just us, but stop and consider how many times your response to an offer of help has been, "Oh, no, that's okay. I'm fine, but I'll let you know!" Yeah, right. Interestingly enough, we were right smack dab in the thick of writing this book when Dardi had a nasty encounter with a portable basketball hoop that got caught in the wind as we were repositioning it to fill the base with water. She ended up laid out right there in the driveway. An emergency room visit and CT scan later, she was fortunate to have her skull intact, but she looked and felt like someone had taken batting practice on her face. Guess what? She pulled out the, "I'll be okay" card when Joe's mom offered to come stay with her because he was scheduled to leave in a couple days for a business trip. Joe promptly responded with, "You just finished telling people to accept kindness and care from others; follow your own advice." Ouch. Dardi confesses, "I relented, and the truth is it was wonderful to have her help. My mother-in-law kept the kids fed and in clean clothes and allowed me to rest, which as much as I hate to admit it, I needed." It really is okay to hang our super hero capes up and be the recipient of a caring gesture, so just say yes even when your inner prideful punk tells you to do otherwise. Don't deprive yourself or the person offering to come alongside you the opportunity to have a caring connection.

Your yes might feel rusty, tired, afraid, uncertain, or even broken, but start using it anyway. Be intentional with saying yes to smaller things; you don't have to agree to trek across Europe with a backpack, but hey, who knows! Saying yes may feel vulnerable, but ultimately, it allows for experiences that can be empowering, encouraging, or that we can laugh about the nonsense or even their level of failure, but the bottom line is, it's living. It's being. It's pushing our way out of the mundane box we can so easily find ourselves mushed into, and it feels ever so good to stretch.

We were remembering several years ago, our son, who was a freshman in high school at the time, was into this crazy teenage game called "What are the Odds?" The details are a bit fuzzy, but it involved a dare, guessing something, and then completing the dare if you lost. We were walking in downtown Charleston, South Carolina, while visiting our daughter when our son put Mom up to it. Her first inclination was no way. No. Way. This was not her first rodeo with teenage shenanigans, but something about the look of expectation on her family's faces made her rethink her stance. She had decided the odds were in her favor anyway, so she felt fairly confident this would end well for her. It actually ended with her standing in the middle of a fountain in street clothes in downtown Charleston in front of her husband, her children, and a multitude of onlooking strangers.

We know that's a silly, random story you'd probably have to witness to fully appreciate, but the point is it's truly one of Dardi's most favorite moments ever, and she almost missed it. Not exercising our yes can not only deny us of an experience, but it can also deny the creation of memories with people we care about.

Self-Care Strategy #7: Be Intentional with Kindness Toward Others

We suppose it could feel contradictory to speak of self-care and being intentional with kindness toward others, but hang in there with us. Human beings are wired for connection. We are not meant to live this life alone, but let's face it, in this day and age of technology, we've never been more virtually connected and more lonely all at once. From dinner tables to city sidewalks to ball games, you can find people with their heads down staring into the abyss of a mobile device instead of being fully present with the people surrounding them. We've already discussed the multitude of reasons to unplug, but let's dig into why simply but intentionally investing in others can boost our emotional well-being and be one of the best self-care strategies we can utilize. According to an article by Nelson, Layous, Cole, and Lyubomirsky (2016), a study published in *Clinical Psychological Science* found when we help others, we can also help ourselves. A cohort of people reported helping others boosted their daily well-being. A greater number of selfless acts were linked to higher levels of daily positive emotion and better overall mental health. The participants' helping behavior also influenced how they responded to stress. Helping others seemed to buffer the negative effects of stress on well-being.

If you want to get technical, random acts of kindness are dope. Dopamine, that is. "Performing random acts of kindness helps boost your psychological health by activating the release of dopamine, the feel-good neurotransmitter in the brain, often referred to as a 'helper's high.' This is based on the theory that giving produces endorphins in the brain that mimic a morphine high. Simply being motivated by generosity can benefit you as much as it does those receiving your help" (Nelson et al., 2016). Being intentional with random acts of kindness is not at all meant to crush the healthy boundaries created by learning to say no. Instead, it's meant to be a simple practice of engagement in the world around you that benefits your sense of connectivity and purpose. You can certainly perform random acts of kindness on a large scale if you're so inclined, but seriously, you can do something as simple as saying a few kind words that pop into your head, which takes all of thirty seconds, and the positive ramifications could last you and the recipient for hours. However, note that we said it could possibly last for hours, not days or forever, which is why this is a practice and not a one-time gig. Dr. Waguih William IsHak, a professor of psychiatry at Cedars-Sinai explains, "…kindness is most beneficial as a practice—something we work into our daily routine whether in the form of volunteer work, dropping coins into an expired parking meter, bringing a snack to share with your office mates, or holding the elevator for someone. The rewards of acts of kindness are many. Acts of kindness help us feel better and they help those who receive them. We're building better selves and better communities at the same time" (2019). So, whether it's with your students, your coworkers, your family, or a simple kind word or gesture to a stranger, keep practicing! Your neurotransmitters will thank you.

Self-Care Strategy #8: It's Not a Competition

This is probably going to be short and sweet, so here goes. Stop measuring yourself and your gifts against what you see online or in the classroom next door. As far as we're concerned, this is a huge component to self-care because if we get caught up in the comparison game, we will find ourselves feeling less than, discontent, doubtful, and a whole web of other untruths. It was recently brought to our attention that there's a website where people are sharing their classroom transformations. It's like the educational version of one of those house flipping reality TV shows, but instead of houses going through a remodel, classrooms are being overhauled into an educational oasis. You know what? If that's your thing, your gift, your love language, then that's awesome! However, if you see a picture of someone's classroom looking magical and feel burdened to create a land of unicorns, stop. Their thing doesn't need to be your thing. If your classroom or office is a mish mash of pieces parts but you love slipping notes of encouragement to students, that's every bit as beautiful. If your educational love language is taking kids outside for an impromptu nature walk, amazing. If you have the gift of being present for kids, be it a listening ear or a fan at their extracurricular, it is appreciated. Brown states, "Stay in your lane. Comparison kills creativity and joy" (2015). Ultimately, your individuality and your care are what your students will remember, no matter what form it takes. Ditch the measuring stick and be you.

Self-Care Strategy #9: Laugh

Life isn't very funny sometimes, that's for sure. It's easy for our sense of humor to get lost in the mix of stress, weariness, and the rigors of life, but it's a proven fact that laughter is not only a good thing, but it is beneficial to our overall well-being. Ben-Moshe (2017) lists seven reasons laughter is important:

1. *Builds resilience:* Learning to laugh at yourself assists in adjusting to stress and adversity.
2. *Creates a positive mindset:* Laughter orients the brain to a positive mindset—regular laughter and smiling actually changes the brain's chemistry through neuroplasticity.
3. *Enhances communication and connects people:* It's very hard for two people who laugh together to feel any animosity toward each other. It's a fantastic team builder.
4. *Reduces stress:* Laughter helps shift difficult emotions, freeing the body and mind of stress.
5. *Frees the mind to be more creative and productive:* Laughter has a similar effect on the brain as meditation, bringing you very much into the present moment.

6. *Increases oxygenation:* This optimizes healthy body and brain functioning, improving concentration and productivity levels.
7. *Promotes playfulness:* Enhancing imagination, cognitive and emotional strength, and also interaction with others.

Another article by Robinson, Smith, and Segal (2018) lists the following benefits of laughter:

Physical health benefits of laughter:

- Boosts immunity
- Lowers stress hormones
- Decreases pain
- Relaxes your muscles
- Prevents heart disease

Mental health benefits of laughter:

- Adds joy and zest to life
- Eases anxiety and tension
- Relieves stress
- Improves mood
- Strengthens resilience

Social benefits of laughter:

- Strengthens relationships
- Attracts others to us
- Enhances teamwork
- Helps defuse conflict
- Promotes group bonding

Our family often instigates Joe into telling "war stories" from his years in education because some of them are so wildly outrageous that they get everyone laughing until they cry. Educators seem to have chosen a crazy profession that often provides new comedic material at the drop of a hat. Obviously in the moment it's not always laughable, but you must admit that if you don't laugh with the situation when appropriate, you'll end up in a bad state of affairs. We could probably write a whole book documenting Joe's wild ride as an educator, but one story still makes everyone laugh every time someone prods him into telling it.

Joe was a principal at a rural high school, and he came home one day with one of those looks where you know it had been an interesting day. He proceeded to explain that he had been conducting interviews for an open teaching position when right in the middle of one of the interviews, a student came busting through his office door in a frenzy. This young man jumped up on a chair in front of the interviewee, leaned over, blew a fart, climbed out the open office window, and took off running! By the time Joe arrived outside, the student in question had somehow wrangled himself a baton and decided to exhibit his drum major skills with the band that was practicing during the last period of the day. That kid was leading that band like a boss! Truly, you can't make this stuff up, and you certainly can't predict it will ever happen! Joe recalls, "At that same school, I showed up for my very first day as the head principal only to find a deer staring me down from the other end of the hallway. The only thing between me and him was a newly waxed floor. All I could see was the headline 'Deer Destroys High School while Head Principal Looks On.' I mean, what do you do with that? Thankfully, a student way more deer-savvy arrived on the scene and helped usher that animal back out the door it came through without it tearing up the place." Given the same scenarios, anyone would most certainly have every right to be in a complete twist of frustration or anger about either one of those situations. However, it's just better to laugh at the absurdity of thinking any professional training could ever possibly prepare you for this! And on the plus side, our family seems to fully appreciate the caliber of entertainment that evolves from a day in the life of an educator.

If you feel like your sense of humor is missing in action, here are a few suggestions from Robinson et al., (2018) for developing your sense of humor:

- *Laugh at yourself:* Share your embarrassing moments. The best way to take yourself less seriously is to talk about times when you took yourself too seriously.
- *Attempt to laugh at situations rather than bemoan them:* Look for the humor in a bad situation and uncover the irony and absurdity of life. When something negative happens, try to make it a humorous anecdote that will make others laugh.
- *Don't dwell on the negative:* Try to avoid negative people and don't dwell on news stories, entertainment, or conversations that make you sad or unhappy. Many things in life are beyond your control—particularly the behavior of other people.
- *Find your inner child:* Pay attention to children and try to emulate them—after all, they are the experts on playing, taking life lightly, and laughing at ordinary things.
- *Don't go a day without laughing:* Think of it like exercise or breakfast and make a conscious effort to find something each day that makes you laugh. Set aside ten to fifteen minutes and do something that amuses you. The more you get used to laughing each day, the less effort you'll have to make.

According to American writer Mark Twain, "Humanity has unquestionably one really effective weapon—laughter. Power, money, persuasion, supplication, persecution—these can lift at a colossal humbug—push it a little—weaken it a little, century by century, but only laughter can blow it to rags and atoms at a blast. Against the assault of laughter nothing can stand" (1916). Laugh lines are beautiful, so make sure you're creating them. But truly, laughter is an amazing tool in our self-care arsenal.

Self-Care Strategy #10: Know When to Say When

Many of us at one time or another have probably seen a recap of a marathon runner getting to the very last leg of a race only to have their bodies begin to betray them. Their legs start to buckle, they stumble, and yet, instead of saying, "Ok, I'm done" or "Ok, I need to take a break," they keep going! Rather than thinking through a big picture lens of "this could land me in the hospital, put me flat on my back for days, or at the very least, negatively impact me and my ability to keep running for a very long time," they seem to have tunnel vision only for the task at hand. Doesn't matter that they've hit a wall; doesn't matter the health implications. Just. Keep. Going....

Who does this sound like? If you really don't know the answer, we'll give you a hint: Go take a gander in the mirror. Unless you are brand spanking new to your career, our best guess is that you can relate to this scenario sometime between Spring break and Memorial Day. Some years it might even surface around Thanksgiving break. Joe confesses to experiencing this kind of fatigue on more than one occasion over the years but admits to his steadfast commitment to keep giving his all anyway.

Dardi recalls, "Several years ago, I had my own bout with this phenomenon. As mentioned earlier in the book, we were foster parents for a few years. At one point, our already large family of seven was entrusted with the care of two six-month-old babies as well as a two-and-a-half-year-old child. One of the babies had been a preemie, and the other two had experienced ongoing neglect, so their care needs were significant. If I wasn't feeding someone, I was changing someone, all while trying to meet their emotional needs, and this was 24-7 in addition to all the other demands of regular family life. To be frank, I was living on minimal sleep and iced coffee, and I had tunnel vision like nobody's business.

One evening, Joe came home from work with a look of determination on his face. He took the baby that was on my hip at that moment and said, 'Go freshen up (which was a kind way of saying you look like death and smell like spit up); Jodi is coming over to take you to dinner. You can't say no.' Remember our point about saying yes to the kindness of others? I already confessed to being highly qualified in the prideful department, but this was another instance where I didn't argue. In hindsight, I had become that marathon runner barely able to stand. Lucky for me, I had someone who stepped in and said, 'Time out.' In my tunnel vision, all I could see was doing the next thing for these children who needed me. What I failed to comprehend in my fatigued stupor was that taking a moment to refresh and regroup would awaken my senses and allow me to better meet their needs, not to mention find some joy in doing so."

Really, this is the epitome of an educator with compassion fatigue. An educator puts the needs of his/her students at the forefront, regardless of what their own personal needs might be. Minds and bodies somehow convince us that if we pause for even a minute to regroup, we are weak or have somehow failed ourselves and others. We teeter on the edge of determination and measuring up to our tendencies toward perfection. Brene Brown suggests, "Understanding the difference between healthy striving and perfectionism is critical to laying down the shield and picking up your life. Research shows that perfectionism hampers success. In fact, it's often the path to depression, anxiety, addiction, and life paralysis" (2010). Dear educator, we hope you are always lucky enough to have someone that issues you a time out when they see you begin to limp. However, it's okay, no it's more than okay, for you to be your own first responder. Be in tune with yourself and know when to say when. Personal growth pioneer Jennifer Louden states, "Self-care is not selfish or self-indulgent. We cannot nurture others from a dry well. We need to take care of our own needs first, so that we can give from our surplus, our abundance. When we nurture others from a place of fullness, we feel renewed instead of taken advantage of" (2005).

You don't need what feels like a justifiable reason to use that personal day (How many of you have only used your personal days when you felt like you could justify it by tending to someone else?). Give yourself permission to take a day to do anything or absolutely nothing; only you can gauge what will fill your tank up a bit. Keep allowing space for the best version of you to be at the forefront of your days. You are worth it.

Self-Care Strategy #11: Do Preventative Maintenance (Get Your Checkups!)

This may seem like a no brainer, but we all lead super busy lives, so it's easy to keep putting things off until tomorrow and somehow feel like they can wait. Most of us are diligent with our children's or pet's preventative checkups, so we need to be sure we're being just as diligent with making ourselves a priority. The Centers for Disease Control & Prevention's (n.d.) website states,

> Nationally, Americans use preventive services at about half the recommended rate. Chronic diseases, such as heart disease, cancer, and diabetes, are responsible for 7 of every 10 deaths among Americans each year and account for 75% of the nation's health spending. These chronic diseases can be largely preventable through close partnership with your healthcare team, or can be detected through appropriate screenings, when treatment works best.
>
> Eating healthy, exercising regularly, avoiding tobacco, and receiving preventive services such as cancer screenings, preventive visits and vaccinations are just a few examples of ways people can stay healthy … And yet, despite the benefits of many preventive health services, too many Americans go without needed preventive care.

Let's not forget the mental health component of our physical health. We've said it before, we'll say it again: Do not be hesitant to seek out professional care with your mental health. According to an article published in *Men's Health,* "Your mental health is inseparable from your physical health. Not a revolutionary concept, but what is astounding is the stigmatization that still surrounds men who dare to talk about their mental struggles" (Evans, 2018). Regardless of gender, don't allow fear to get in the way of your health—mind, body, and soul.

We are not doctors, nor do we play them on television (well, actually, Joe is a doctor, just not a medical doctor!), but from experience we have found that there are also some interesting holistic approaches to physical self-care that can be beneficial when combined with appropriate medical preventative measures and mental health care. In our earlier days, we never would have envisioned suggesting this because things like acupuncture, oils, therapeutic massage, herbal supplements, and chiropractic care seemed a little "out there." We would encourage anyone to not be afraid to investigate the plethora of reputable options to find a combination of health care that works for you! Joe has an extreme aversion to needles, but low and behold, acupuncture has benefitted him on several occasions. Dardi ran her first and only marathon several years back. If it weren't for the intervention of a wonderful chiropractor helping her with a defiant hamstring, she would not have made it to the finish line.

Life is a marathon, friends. Be proactive with your health by staying tuned into what you need, preferably before it becomes an issue. Seek whatever care necessary to cross that finish line. You are your best advocate, so step up for you!

Self-Care Strategy #12: Eat, Sleep, and Move Your Body

We mentioned at the very beginning of this chapter that we get frustrated when eating right, getting enough sleep, and exercise are the immediate go-to for self-care. Anything transformative in life requires proper positioning for that transformation, and we believe that the preceding self-care strategies are a good start to positioning ourselves for building resilience, which really is what the goal of self-care should be. In doing so, we are better equipped to face the inevitable messiness that comes along in different seasons of life. However, we would be remiss if we didn't address these foundational ingredients to a healthy life. The research abounds about why we should strive to eat right, get adequate sleep, and exercise, so instead of quoting a multitude of statistics, we thought we'd share a few of our own tricks and realizations when it comes to these things.

The paradox of our marriage is that one of us has struggled with body image issues while the other has the metabolism of a hummingbird. What this means is that up until the last few years, Joe has dined on cheeseburgers and chocolate while Dardi has dabbled in every diet under the sun. At some point a few years back, we both came to the realization that neither of our approaches to food were healthy or even serving us well, so we decided to find a balance in there. Are we perfect? Absolutely not. Do we eat cake sometimes? Absolutely. We've tried to find a balance that fits real life. We eat our veggies; well, Joe juices his, but we are eating (or drinking) them. However, we also don't go into deprivation mode because that feels like stress, and stress is what we're trying to avoid. Bottom line: Our advice for eating right is to find a healthy balance that works for you, balance being the key word! If you need some assistance, find a nutritionally sound program that feels sustainable to you to help get you headed in the right direction. If you aren't sure what might be best for you, take a few options to your family doctor to get his/her guidance.

"Sleep is overrated." We have no idea who ever said that or why they would say such a thing! Remember, we have raised nine children, seven from infancy, so sleep was an elusive commodity for us for many years. If it hadn't been for Sunday afternoon naps and pinch hitting for one another on those dreadfully early mornings, we aren't sure we'd have survived! Our bodies need rest, but sometimes the demands and/or stresses of life impede our ability to get enough sleep or even sleep at all. While we have yet to hear a tried and true antidote to not sleeping enough or not sleeping well, we have become intentional with a few things to position ourselves for a greater chance at a decent night of sleep:

1. *Make your bed:* Seriously, make your bed the minute you get out of it in the morning before you become busy with everything else. We don't even know if there's anything scientific about this, but from personal experience, we feel like this is imperative to a successful night of rest. If our day has been chaotic or messy, we need to find our way to a mental sanctuary come bedtime. What we don't need is to give our brains the idea that we're exiting one mess to crawl into another. People, we used to use our bed as the laundry folding station for our family of eleven. More often than not, we would forget to tell the crew to get their clothes off our bed and put them away during the day, which would result in an epic grown-up temper tantrum when we'd stumble into our bedroom after a long day. Needless to say, we finally wised up and this practice no longer exists in our house. The point is this: Even if your day or the condition of the rest of your home has gone to heck in a handbasket, when you've made your bed first thing, you'll have a peaceful space waiting for you where you can enjoy some rest.
2. *Go to bed:* This seems to be harder for some than for others. There's always something else to do, something else to watch, one more chapter to read, or more scrolling to do on the Internet. For some people, life is finally quiet, so it feels good to just bask in the glory of not having anyone pulling on you, but you still need to set a reasonable time to go to bed. Otherwise, it's suddenly crunch time

where you're calculating if you go to sleep now, you'll have X number of hours until the alarm is going off. Trying to find rest under pressure doesn't work very well, so if you must, give yourself a bedtime and stick to it.

3. *Don't take junk to bed:* Resolve any conflicts before you go to bed. Put your phone on silent, and then put it down, too. Leave work and the laptop someplace else. If something is going on in your life that has you troubled, take a minute before bed to process it in your journal. We can't tell you the number of times one of us has gone to bed with a heavy heart about something only to find ourselves wide away at 3:00 a.m. with a knot in the stomach. That's an awful predicament because the world is too quiet, and the mind goes a million miles an hour in the wrong direction. If we're smart, we drag our rear out of bed to journal. There's something about throwing out thoughts on paper that can sometimes allow us to "put it down" for a while. It doesn't fix anything, but it seems that by acknowledging that there's something going on and validating the associated feelings, it's easier to temporarily put it down and sleep. Processing it on paper can also help with feeling empowered or gaining a different, more encouraged perspective.

There are always those practical things like avoiding caffeine late in the day, not eating foods before bed that cause you indigestion, or not falling asleep with the light or television still on that are good rules of thumb for finding a healthy sleep routine. There are also some environmental things like white noise machines or an essential oil diffuser that people utilize. We just recently started using a diffuser ourselves with lavender oil; we don't know if it's helping anything, but we love the smell and it adds to that peaceful, sanctuary feeling!

Additionally, there are medical interventions available. If you feel that your sleep, or lack of sleep, is having a negative effect on your health, it's important to investigate the reason with a doctor to see if a medical intervention may be necessary for you to get back on track.

Now let's talk about the need for exercise. Exercising isn't just a necessary evil for fitting into one's pants. We've come to realize it's just plain necessary. First, it's necessary for our physical health, but just as important, it's necessary for our mental health. We came to this conclusion again after a couple of cross country moves. As we mentioned before, we moved from Ohio to Florida as we stepped into our business full-time. We found a lovely place in Florida to rent for that season of our life which accommodated both our family and our two boxers. The only downside was that there was no fenced backyard. Out of necessity, we had to walk the boxers a minimum of three times per day for potty breaks and to keep our relationship with our doggies a sane one (a tired boxer is a well-behaved boxer). After a couple years, we decided to make the move back home to Ohio, and our new home has a fenced backyard. Between the weather fluctuations that occur in Ohio in the Spring (in case you are unaware, one can experience all four seasons in just one day in this fickle climate), the busyness involved in transitioning to a new community, and the fact that we could now simply open the back door to let the dogs out, we were no longer taking our regular walks. We both remember one day looking at each other and saying, "I feel like crap." It wasn't just "my pants are too tight, I feel like crap," but it was an overall feeling of being overwhelmed and grumpy. It finally dawned on us that we were no longer experiencing the mental breaks that those walks provided. Granted, those walks provided physical benefits, but they also provided that quiet space we mentioned earlier in this chapter where we could either think or not think at all.

We've run the gamut of exercise routines over the years. Between the two of us, we've done step aerobics, trained for a marathon, yoga, karate, and what feels like everything in between. Somewhere we read that pulling weeds counts as exercise, but neither of us think much of that for our mental health and well-being. Right now, we've been walking and hiking with some interval and strength training mixed in, but the important thing is it's something. That's really the point…find something or a combination of somethings that gets your blood pumping and gives you space to think, or not, and find some enjoyment in it, too! If it feels like a chore (like flower beds feel to us, but Dardi's grandmother would have said otherwise), try a new thing, and keep trying new things, until you find something that you look forward to and enjoy. It may even vary by season, but keep that body moving to benefit your mind, body, and soul!

As we wrap up this chapter, we want to emphasize that this list of twelve strategies is not intended to come across like an overwhelming "to-do" list. Remember at the beginning of the chapter we said, "It's not about guilt; it's about vision." Instead of trying to implement every single strategy immediately, maybe pick three that you feel might be most beneficial to you in this season of life and build from there. Identify the strategies you are already doing well and congratulate yourself! If you think any of the suggestions are bunk, that's totally okay, too. Tuck those away for later because it's funny how our needs can change over time. Every one of us is on a unique personal journey, so our hope is that these strategies are a springboard for you to find your strength, your incredible value, and your resilience for the journey.

Personal Self-Care Strategies at a Glance

- Journal
- Choose your words wisely
- Know your triggers
- Unplug
- Learn to say no
- Learn to say yes
- Be intention with kindness toward others

- It's not a competition
- Laugh
- Know when to say when
- Do preventative maintenance (get your checkups!)
- Eat, sleep, and move your body

Reading, Reflection, and Discussion Points

1. What kind of "season" do you feel like you're in now?
2. As an educator, what do you recall as your best season? What do you recall as your most challenging season? Are there any similarities or differences between the two?
3. What kinds of feelings and/or attitudes did your best and most challenging seasons in education bring about?
4. How do you think journaling might benefit you as you pursue health and well-being?
5. Have you ever considered the power of your internal dialogue? Do you feel this is a strength or challenge point for you?
6. Consider your story, every single part. Fill in the blank with empowerment: I am __________.

   Group team building activity: Divide your group as appropriate if it is large. We suggest creating teams of people that have a familiar working relationship with others on their team. If your group is smaller, stay in one group. Pass out index cards and label one card at a time with a team member's name until you have a card labeled for each person. For each team member, write a statement of appreciation about a strength you've witnessed in them, a character trait you admire in them, kindness you've experienced from them, or whatever comes to mind. Be brief, concise, and sincere (example: You are a strong advocate for kids). When finished, each person will receive their cards to read. Tuck the cards you receive away for when you need a dose of truth or get some of your artistically gifted people to create an empowerment collage in the break room.

7. At the beginning of this book, we mentioned that seventy-one percent of submissions we examined from participants in our online course stated that one of their biggest challenge points was being aware of compassion fatigue and the need for self-care. The second highest response (sixty-seven percent) as a challenge point was being aware of one's triggers. Are you cognizant of your personal triggers? If so, do you have practiced responses that have been helpful? If not, do you think identifying your triggers and having practiced responses would benefit you personally and professionally?
8. How has technology and the Internet enhanced your life and job?
9. How has technology and the Internet been detrimental to your life and job?
10. Does saying no to other's requests make you feel guilty? If so, how might you readjust your thinking about "no" being a healthy boundary? Food for thought: Do you take it personally if someone says no to you?
11. When was the last time you said yes to something outside your comfort zone? How do you feel looking back on it?
12. Think back on a time someone unexpectedly did or said something kind for/to you. How could you pay it forward within the next week?
13. Do you find that you pull out the "measuring stick" in any area of your personal or professional life?
14. How's your sense of humor? Do you find it's more intact at either home or work?
15. When was the last time you took a refreshing break from life? How are you at gauging when a break is needed?
16. What are you doing for your overall health and wellness?
17. Of these personal self-care strategies, are there three (or more) that you feel are strengths for you? Which three would you classify as challenge points?
18. As you revisit your vision and hope for yourself, how might you add to or adjust it after reading this chapter? How about for your workplace?

Point to ponder: Many of the personal self-care strategies could be woven into the fabric of your classroom or school setting with your students, as well. Modeling self-care strategies and incorporating them into the daily routine can be a wonderful way to position students to develop and practice a healthy attitude toward self and others, thus contributing positively to the overall culture.

References

American Psychological Association. (2001). A new reason for keeping a diary. Retrieved April 2019, from https://www.apa.org/monitor/sep01/keepdiary

Ben-Moshe, R. (2017). *Laughing at cancer: How to heal with love, laughter, and mindfulness.* Ringwood, VIC, Australia: Brolga Publishing Pty Ltd.

Brown, B. (2015). *Rising strong* (1st ed.). New York, NY: Spiegel & Grau, an imprint of Random House.

Brown, C. B. (2010). *The gifts of imperfection: Let go of who you think you're supposed to be and embrace who you are.* Center City, MI: Hazelden.

Brown, C. B. (2012). *Daring greatly: How the courage to be vulnerable transforms the way we live, love, parent, and lead.* New York, NY: Gotham.

Cedars-Sinai Staff. (2019). The science of kindness. Retrieved August 2019, from https://blog.cedars-sinai.edu/science-of-kindness/

Centers for Disease Control & Prevention. (n.d.) Preventative health care. Retrieved May 2019, from https://www.cdc.gov/healthcommunication/toolstemplates/entertainmented/tips/PreventiveHealth.html

Cunningham, L. (2012). Exhaustion is not a status symbol. Retrieved June 2019, from https://www.washingtonpost.com/national/exhaustion-is-not-a-status-symbol/2012/10/02/19d27aa8-0cba-11e2-bb5e-492c0d30bff6_story.html?noredirect=on

Davies, J. (n.d.) What are emotional triggers and how they could be secretly influencing your life. Retrieved June 2019, from https://www.learning-mind.com/what-are-emotional-triggers/

Evans, S. (2018). Not talking about mental health is literally killing men. Retrieved May 2019, from https://www.menshealth.com/health/a20111514/men-mental-health-awareness-month/

Friedman, S. (2014). *Leading the life you want: Skills for integrating work and life*. Boston, MA: Harvard Business School Publishing.

Good Relaxation. (2016). The 3 benefits of positive self-talk. Retrieved April 2019, from https://goodrelaxation.com/2016/05/benefits-of-positive-self-talk/

Holden, R. (2011). *Authentic success: Essential lessons and practices from the world's leading coaching program on success intelligence*. Carlsbad, CA: Hay House.

Janes, B. (2019). Why it's important to schedule more downtime for your brain. Retrieved August 2019, from https://www.shape.com/lifestyle/mind-and-body/why-its-important-schedule-more-downtime-your-brain

Jantz, G. L. (2016). The power of positive self-talk: Working to overwrite the negative voice with positive truths. Retrieved April 2019, from https://www.psychologytoday.com/us/blog/hope-relationships/201605/the-power-positive-self-talk

Kennedy, L. (2002). Spielberg in the twilight zone. Retrieved July 2019, from https://www.wired.com/2002/06/spielberg/

Louden, J. (2005). *The women's comfort book: A self-nurturing guide for restoring balance in your life*. San Francisco, CA: HarperOne.

Marinella, S. (2017). *The story you need to tell: Writing to heal from trauma, illness, or loss*. Novato, CA: New World Library.

Molla, R. (2018). Mary Meeker's 2018 Internet Trends Report. Retrieved April 2019, from https://www.recode.net/2018/5/30/17385116/mary-meeker-slides-internet-trends-code-conference-2018

Nelson, K. S., Layous, K., Cole, S. W., & Lyubomirsky, S. (2016). Do unto others or treat yourself? The effects of prosocial and self-focused behavior on psychological flourishing. *Emotion*, 16(6), 850–861.

Perry, B. D., & Szalavitz, M. (2008). *The boy who was raised as a dog: And other stories from a child psychiatrist's notebook: What traumatized children can teach us about loss, love, and healing*. New York, NY: Basic Books.

Robinson, L., Smith, M., & Segal, J. (2018). Laughter is the best medicine: The health benefits of humor and laughter. Retrieved

May 2019, from https://www.helpguide.org/articles/mental-health/laughter-is-the-best-medicine.htm/

Rowe, A. (n.d.) 7 reasons you should always write down your goal. Retrieved April 2019, from https://thestrive.co/write-down-your-goals/

Shpancer, N. (2010). Emotional acceptance: Why feeling bad is good. Retrieved April 2019, from https://www.psychologytoday.com/us/blog/insight-therapy/201009/emotional-acceptance-why-feeling-bad-is-good

Tugaleva, V. (2017). *The art of talking to yourself: Self-awareness meets the inner conversation.* UK: Soulux Press.

Twain, M. (1916). *The mysterious stranger.* New York, NY: Harper & Brothers Publishers.

Woodrow Wilson Quotes. (n.d.). BrainyQuote.com. Retrieved October 2019, from BrainyQuote.com Web site: https://www.brainyquote.com/quotes/woodrow_wilson_121798

5

Community Connection: Professional Strategies for Self-Care

Several years back, Dardi traveled to two different countries for two weeks each time. Aside from the usual homesickness, her first trip was extremely enjoyable for her as she encountered so many amazing people and was exposed to an array of experiences. However, her second trip to a different country was another story. She recalls feeling very alone and very discouraged by her encounters each day. She readily admits that she was sour on the whole experience and had a major meltdown over her feelings of distress and isolation. The turning point for her came during some processing time in her journal and with Joe. She remembers reading back through her words and realizing that every single thing she focused on was about all of the external negatives. However, she had written nothing about any positives or anything she had tried to accomplish that resembled who she is as a person. She was becoming a product of her surroundings instead of countering the adversity with looking for and finding positives or doing anything to feel like herself. Dardi is a very relational person, so she set out the next day to conduct herself in a way that felt edifying to who she is. She didn't speak the same language, so she began holding the door for people, making eye contact and sharing a smile, and she even asked to get a picture with the waitresses she had fumbled her way through ordering food with over several days in the restaurant next door to her hotel. Granted, not every initiative was received with a mutuality—she readily admits that some people looked at her like she had a third eye—but other responses were extremely pleasant. That request for a picture with her waitresses sent the whole place into a flurry of excitement with everyone getting their phones to snap their own pictures to capture this momentous occasion. They were thrilled by a simple request for connection. "Ye cannot live for yourselves; a thousand fibres connect you with your fellow-men, and along those fibres, as along sympathetic threads, run your actions as causes, and return to you as effects" (Melvill, 1855) was spoken so many years ago, yet it beautifully illustrates our need for connection as well as the incredible opportunity we have to contribute to our own well-being by being mindful of what we put forth into our workplace in anticipation of what we will receive in return. We began envisioning this in Chapter 3, so let's continue moving forward in bringing more definition to that vision.

As an educator, have you ever found yourself in a culture where you didn't seem to fit or even speak the same language and where you felt like you were just trying to get through it? Joe has, more than once. Being an educator whose fundamental belief is that we need to keep kids in school, look for redeeming qualities, practice restorative justice, increase esteem, and extend grace whenever possible while considering extenuating circumstances, he's felt like the oddball out in cultures where the practice was grounded in fear, retaliation, and control. Joe was even passed over for a job promotion once because he refused to lead by force and fear. Let's not sugarcoat anything: It's not easy to be immersed in a place where you feel like you're swimming upstream every single day, and there may come a point where you must make a decision to find employment somewhere else if there's no attempt at remediation in sight. However, don't lose yourself in the meantime. Don't put who you are and what you do on hold in anticipation of being in a place that might be a better fit. Release yourself from the burden of looking outward at everything that's flawed; feel empowered as you look inward and unleash all that is right. You just may be the spark that ignites the change you wish to see.

The burden of self-care should not be carried alone unless you happen to live an isolated existence. Not hardly, right? Educators spend a minimum of 260 days as a community member in their workplace; most days, they spend more waking hours there than with their families. One of the number one complaints we hear from educators today has nothing to do with their students. Instead, they feel unhappy in their workplace. According to Podolsky, Kini, Bishop, and Darling-Hammond (2016), the top three potentially adverse conditions consistently cited by educators are:

1. *School leadership and administrative support:* Administrative support is often the top reason that teachers identify for leaving or staying in the profession, or in a given school, outweighing even salary considerations for some teachers.
2. *Opportunities for professional collaboration and shared decision-making:* Teachers' career decisions are shaped by their connectedness to a team working toward a common shared purpose. Opportunities for teacher collaboration and input are key factors.
3. *Accountability systems:* Approximately twenty-five percent of public school teachers who left the profession in 2012 reported that dissatisfaction with the influence of school assessment and accountability measures on their teaching or curriculum was extremely or very important

> in their decision to leave. Many teachers have said that the focus on testing, test preparation, and a narrower, mandated curriculum has reduced their ability to teach in ways they feel are more effective.

Combine these issues with some of the concerns listed in our "Who?" and "What?" are we trying to change, and it's no wonder educators feel like the walking wounded, stumbling into their workplace every day. A person could be diligently incorporating the strategies listed in the previous chapter only to still feel a sense of depletion.

Here's what we believe beyond a shadow of a doubt: The perception of self-care is an anomaly. Its very name suggests that the burden of emotional and mental well-being falls on self alone, but the reality is, we need one another to experience wholeness and change. Not only that, we don't live in a bubble where we have no one else to consider, thus having complete control over our atmosphere. But if we can only control ourselves, how do we handle everything going on around us? We must make an intentional investment in relational equity in order to find health, hope, and healing on a personal and organizational level. Nakita Valerio, a Toronto-based community organizer and researcher, states, "Shouting 'self-care' at people who actually need 'community care' is how we fail people" (2019).

We are in a people business that revolves around human capital. We each must be deliberate with our thoughts and interactions toward not only self, but others in order to breach the chasm between isolation and a sense of community. Dr. Bruce Perry states, "Relationships matter; the currency for systemic change is trust, and trust comes through forming healthy relationships. People, not programs, change people" (Perry & Szalavitz, 2008). Further, Mother Teresa has said, "If we have no peace, it is because we have forgotten that we belong to each other" (n.d.).

As we've mentioned previously, you cannot control other people, but you can become a positive influence with the people around you. If every one of us is thoughtfully considering how our presence contributes to the overall culture, we can begin filling our spaces with compassion, positivity, authenticity, and empathetic connections. If people are attracted to your attitude and behavior, they are bound to be impacted and influenced by it, as well, and we can begin the task of eradicating toxic work environments, which would serve all of us well as we seek a sense of wholeness.

Professional Self-Care Strategy #1: Be a Trusted Colleague

We suspect that you've heard of an "open door policy," but what does that really look like? Joe has always prided himself on being accessible whether he was teaching, coaching, working in administration, or even now as he's out speaking at conferences or working with schools through professional development. Looking back, there were times he admits he was probably accessible to a fault, which put him in a position of not having healthy boundaries. You can absolutely be accessible and still have healthy boundaries. Practically speaking, it's necessary to find that balance in order to effectively manage professional responsibilities while not sacrificing personal relationships in the process. Joe shares, "If I'm being really honest, there was an instance that I hated to say I didn't have time for someone that was notorious for eating up an hour with small talk. Instead of politely saying I didn't have time at that moment, I hid in my office while my administrative assistant seemed puzzled as she told him she had no idea where I was (and she really didn't because I was hiding in my office). Don't hold that against me. I was a young administrator that needed to learn the art of saying, 'Bill, I'm so sorry. I'd love to catch up with you and hear about all the great work the booster club is doing, but it will have to be another day because I have several pressing matters that I need to complete before an approaching deadline.'"

So, an open-door policy should look like accessibility, and over the years we've also observed that you can say you're accessible, but do you also give the impression of being approachable? It's just a guess, but we've all probably met people that come across as either intimidating or about as approachable as a porcupine. The vibe they give is uncomfortable. The funny thing is, there are many times these very people have no idea that's how they come across. When you really get to know them, you find they're human, too. If you get the feeling that people behave around you like they've just been called to the principal's office, you may want to check your approachability factor.

Accessibility, approachability, and what? There's a third piece that is critical to the whole equation: Be a safe place. Just as our students need to feel like they have safe places to be themselves, so do adults. Be that place. Be the colleague who knows how to listen. Be the person who knows how to laugh. Be the one who can be objective, and even the one who can offer constructive feedback. Be that person who's willing to step in when someone else needs to step out for a moment. Van der Kolk states, "Being able to feel safe with other people is probably the single most important aspect of mental health; safe connections are fundamental to meaningful and satisfying lives" (2014). You don't have to fix anyone; you don't have to take on the world, either. But be a trusted colleague. As more and more people step into the role of being a trusted colleague, we begin the process of bridging the gap of mistrust and disconnectedness in our workplaces to becoming a healthy community.

Professional Self-Care Strategy #2: Avoid Negative Interactions

A vital component to being a trusted colleague is the need to avoid negative interactions, so much so that it deserves its own bullet point. Negativity will suck the life out of a person and erect barriers to relationships faster than anything else. Negativity can take on lots of forms: Complaining, gossiping, and criticizing with no substance are but a few of its most common denominators. There are certainly instances where issuing a complaint to effect real and positive change is an appropriate exchange with the proper entity. However, when complaining and criticizing are nothing more than rumination with no productive outcome, they serve no purpose except to feed a culture of toxicity. One article states:

> For centuries, researchers have studied the tendency for people to unconsciously and automatically mimic the emotional expressions of others, and in many cases actually feel the same feelings simply by exposure to emotions in social interactions. Studies have found that the mimicry of a frown or a smile or other kinds of emotional expression trigger reactions in our brains that cause us to interpret those expressions as our own feelings. Simply put, as a species, we are innately vulnerable to "catching" other people's emotions. (Carter, 2012)

Don't allow negativity to become a contagion. Redirect conversations that begin to head in the wrong direction, or it's more than okay to excuse yourself from any interaction that is not uplifting, constructive, or appropriate in nature. Maya Angelou shared, "You are the sum total of everything you've ever seen, heard, eaten, smelled, been told, forgot–it's all there. Everything influences each of us, and because of that I try to make sure that my experiences are positive."

Professional Self-Care Strategy #3: You Can't Care Too Much

Do not confuse negative interactions with empathic connections. Life is hard, so if a colleague is struggling, do not shy away from stepping into the proverbial ditch to be a listening ear.

At one point in Joe's career while serving as an administrator, he had someone bark at him, "You care too much!" as if it was a character flaw. Caring and being empathetic is an emotional investment, and the truth of the matter is, it can make us feel uncomfortable, hard feelings. However, the opposite of caring is indifference, and as we discussed in the first chapter, the last thing this world needs is more indifference. As human beings, we are designed to feel and to connect with others. Regarding empathy, Szalavitz and Perry (2010) write,

> By understanding and increasing just this one capacity of the human brain, an enormous amount of social change can be fostered. Failure to understand and cultivate empathy, however, could lead to a society in which no one would want to live—a cold, violent, chaotic, and terrifying war of all against all. This destructive type of culture has appeared repeatedly in various times and places in human history and still reigns in some parts of the world. And it's a culture that we could be inadvertently developing throughout America if we do not address current trends in child rearing, education, economic inequality, and our core values."

Here are some suggestions for cultivating a caring, empathic environment:

1. *Position yourself to care:* By positioning, we mean do you convey an open door policy? Do you ask questions in a way that promotes conversation versus making people feel defensive? Asking "what" questions instead of "why" questions gives space for others to give you a better view of the whole picture about where another person may be coming from in any given situation.
2. *Listen to hear instead of listening to fix:* Many of us are fixers by nature. If there's a problem, let's fix it, but most times, it's

not as simple as that. If you're having a conversation with a colleague and you've opened the door with a "tell me more" question, dial in and listen. It's easy for our brains to jump ahead into a problem-solving mode without being in the moment and hearing the full story. Most people aren't looking to be fixed; they're looking to be heard.

3. *Do not minimize another's feelings:* It also tends to be in our nature to want to alleviate a person's struggle, but by doing so with statements like, "at least this didn't happen" or "yeah, but it could have been worse" statements, we can end up minimizing their feelings instead. Even if you perceive that you might not respond to the same situation with the same feelings, respect that we all respond to things differently. A better response would be, "I can see that this is really hard for you" to validate what another person is experiencing.
4. *Be present and observant within your community of people:* We are certain that multitasking is a prerequisite to working with children. There are always many, many things to think, decisions to make, crises to avert, and plans to be made, and that's just within the first hour of a Monday morning. Attuning to the people around us can simply fall by the wayside as we are navigating all the to-do's within a day, but attunement is a necessary ingredient to fundamentally redesigning professional work cultures. Attunement "describes how reactive a person is to another's emotional needs and moods. A person who is well attuned will respond with appropriate language and behaviors based on another person's emotional state. They are good at recognizing moods and emotions in another person and adapting their own response in accordance" (Attunement, n.d.). Attunement allows us to connect with the people around us, which is critical at a time when children and adults alike are experiencing more and more feelings of disconnection. In an

interview with author Brene Brown, Dan Schawbel (2017) poses the question, "Why do we currently have a crisis of disconnection in our society?" Her reply:

> "…If I had to identify one core variable that magnifies our compulsion to sort ourselves into factions while at the same time cutting ourselves off from real connection with other people, my answer would be fear. Fear of vulnerability. Fear of getting hurt. Fear of the pain of disconnection. Fear of criticism and failure. Fear of conflict. Fear of not measuring up. When we ignore fear and deny vulnerability, fear grows and metastasizes. We move away from a belief in common humanity and unifying change and move into blame and shame. We will do anything that gives us a sense of more certainty and we will give our power to anyone who can promise easy answers and give us an enemy to blame."

When considering the "you care too much" accusation and then reading the above response from Dr. Brown, it shines much light on the situation. Joe reflects, "I was immersed in a culture of fear that had become an attitude of indifference to others, and by going against the grain, I was threatening their fabricated sense of security." This is worth repeating: You CANNOT care too much. It may feel vulnerable, but vulnerability allows us to be real, to feel, and to be human, which is exactly what our workplace needs.

Professional Self-Care Strategy #4: Assume Competence

Just recently, our son, Kade, came home from college for a visit. One of his former high school classmates came to stay at the house for a few days during that visit, and we spent a lot of time reminiscing about their days together on the football field. Our son was a quarterback his freshman year of high school, and his friend was a wide receiver. One play in particular remains in all of our memories. Our son took a snap in shotgun, dropped back a few more steps for a pass, and right before he was leveled by a couple of defensive linemen, he launched a very long pass that looked like it was going to over shoot his target by several yards. Instead, his friend recalls looking back and upon seeing the intense defensive pressure on Kade, kicked into high gear "because I knew Kade was going to put it out there for me, so I better hurry up." Kade recollects, "I knew he'd get there, so I sent it long so he could keep his stride and score." They were both right; pass complete, touchdown scored!

We all need to be good teammates, trusting one another's competence in our respective positions. Sure, everyone makes mistakes, and everyone has room to grow, but to create healthy places where good things are accomplished, we need to assume competence in one another. Trust affords teammates the opportunity to shine, and even more, it creates an environment conducive to courage and creativity. If we are always worried that we are going to be ridiculed or questioned, the morale of our entire professional culture is diminished. To the contrary, assuming competence creates a sense of trust, which in turn contributes to a sense of safety, confidence, and an overall cohesiveness increasing morale. Covey states, "Trust is the glue of life. It's the most essential ingredient in effective communication. It's the foundational principle that holds all relationships" (2004).

Professional Self-Care Strategy #5: Utilize Your Gifts

Have you ever had one of those moments when you run into one of your students outside of school and they look at you in total bewilderment like you don't belong anywhere but at school? It's as if kids think you live at the school, and your life is limited to your content area. Have you ever considered that we, too, unintentionally forget a bit, or even a lot, of our identity outside of the job description?

You are a unique, talented, well-educated individual. You bring a skill set to your team that is different than anyone else's. Lest you think we're about to bust out in a chorus of "This Little Light of Mine," we assure you that we will not. It's not in either of our skill sets or creative giftings. But we will tell you that we've seen it time and again where people start functioning on autopilot. Check the boxes, get it done, repeat. This may work if you're on the assembly line building cars, but we're not building cars. We're building relationships with children. We're contributing to a community of potential world changers. We have the opportunity to equip the next generation with a well-rounded perspective based on the uniqueness of their educational influences.

As a vital part of this equation, ask yourself if you are putting forth all of who you are, or if you've gotten into the habit of living in survival mode. Survival mode may feel safe and like self-preservation, but in reality, being in that mode can be a barrier to relationships with your students and your colleagues. Not only that, it isn't very fun.

Why do you suppose we've lost a bit of ourselves? There's probably a myriad of answers which might include becoming performance driven (tunnel vision), fear of making mistakes, fear of being judged, feeling disconnected, no motivation to collaborate… We're sure the list goes on, but it's worth considering personally and collectively within our organizations. Ultimately, it's possible we've forgotten how to have fun and be ourselves. Regarding the pressure to win in youth sports, an article in *Psychology Today* states,

> It seems logical that creating a fun environment would be likely to enhance enjoyment levels, but in addition to this, it appears that coach-athlete interactions and integrating activities that athletes perceive as enjoyable

> may also have a positive impact on preparation and, ultimately, performance. Preparing fully, in any context, is difficult to do if we are not enjoying the journey that we are on. When we are experiencing an element of pleasure, we tend to push ourselves harder, focus more, and have a greater overall sense of satisfaction.
>
> Wood, 2016

We believe this sentiment transcends from sports to any environment where adults are trying to guide children to be their very best. It would stand to reason that since we are all lifelong learners, we would benefit as adults from bringing a bit of ourselves to the party every day. Dardi shares, "One of my best memories is from fifth grade. Everyone was so intimidated by Ms. Countrymen and dreaded the thought of being assigned to her classroom for the year. Sure enough, I ended up on her class list. I was a shy kid and extremely afraid of getting into trouble, so I didn't have a great outlook on the year with this seemingly stern woman. Right after school began, all of the teachers in fifth and sixth grade collaborated to do 'Fun Fridays.' Each teacher offered mini-classes where they taught the basics for one of their hobbies. One person was teaching chess, another person was doing some type of woodworking, but the mini-class I chose was knitting with Ms. Countrymen. She took time to show us some of her amazing knitted creations, and I was able to learn some basics and knit a blue and white scarf that I proudly gifted to my grandpa. Even more fun was getting to know Ms. Countrymen in that element, and I remember she came to life in a new way, too. She ended up being one of my favorite teachers ever once I got to know her."

Kids thrive on connection; adults do, too. Rediscover and utilize your gifts, your quirks, the things that make you uniquely you, and allow them to be the conduit to having fun again and building a community that knows how to connect and smile.

Professional Self-Care Strategy #6: Be a Mentor—Find a Mentor

More and more schools have begun to implement or expand professional adult mentoring programs. Unfortunately, it appears that sometimes there's a misconception that mentoring equates to someone having a weakness they need assistance in overcoming. If a culture is already struggling to be positive and healthy, it could feel vulnerable to be mentored if this is how mentoring is construed.

To be honest, neither of us view mentoring this way at all. While we concede that it can be an effective strategy to assist new or struggling staff members with challenge points, we also believe it can be so much more. Mentoring can be the difference between isolation and community. It can be the segue for inspiration and encouragement as well as constructive feedback. Anymore, mentoring can and should be a two-way street where we can glean things mutually. Heaven knows, a veteran teacher of twenty-five years may fully appreciate an explanation of some of the new, confounded methods that seem to keep appearing that are the latest, greatest thing for teaching math and reading. (We may be speaking more as a parents here that have attempted to help with homework recently.) And obviously, a rookie teacher would benefit greatly from someone who's been around the block a few times. Education is a stressful occupation, and we are losing too many professionals in their first five years on the job. Mentoring folks that are buckling under the burden does not require you to shoulder their load or feel inadequate because you don't have an answer to the demands. Maybe that's the answer right there. For a new educator, it might be as simple as being empathetic with their feelings by sharing the ways you truly know how they feel, validating them in those feelings, and letting them know they aren't the only one to ever feel that way.

In the end, the greatest benefit of mentoring is relationships. Healthy, honest, mutual relationships make a stronger team and a healthier culture. As educators who spend much time pouring into students, it might prove challenging to find the time. This is when creativity is a must, and this is one of the times technology can be an excellent tool. Be intentional with finding some time to check in, even if it's via text or e-mail. We both have mentoring relationships with people we trust and respect, but due to the unconventional nature of our work and family life, those relationships tend to be fostered creatively. They still work because even if it's regular texts and occasional phone calls with the treat of an in-person coffee date thrown in the mix, they are intentional and meaningful nonetheless.

If for some reason you don't have access to someone you feel you can have a mentoring relationship with in your workplace (for instance, you'd really like to connect with someone in a content area that is specialized), this is where social media can be utilized for something constructive. Anymore, you can access all different types of support systems and groups online with other likeminded professionals. Regardless of where you find a mentoring relationship, be sure each person strives to emulate the very best qualities of an educator as well as exemplify the practice of the previously listed strategies. Guard yourselves from the relationship becoming an emotional dumping ground; instead, seek to be positive, authentic, encouraging, objective, and to work toward solutions if problems are identified.

Professional Self-Care Strategy #7: Forgive

Please note that we saved this one for last. It's been saved for last not because we feel it's the most important, which it may be, but because it's one Joe has struggled with professionally the most. Joe shares, "If I'm being fully transparent, I'm still a work in progress. I know what it's like to feel trapped in a toxic work culture, to feel thrown under the bus, to feel like my integrity has been questioned, to feel demeaned and demoralized, or to feel like I've in some way failed a student or colleague. Unfortunately, this seems to be the norm rather than the exception in too many environments, and there don't seem to be many professionals who get through their careers unscathed. Dardi and I have weathered a few storms along the way, and maybe that's why the forgiveness piece is so difficult. The toxicity didn't just affect me; it seeped into my family and even felt like a threat to my livelihood, which in turn felt like a threat to my family's wellbeing." We are going to delve deeper into toxic environments shortly, but we needed to touch on it here to lay the foundation for why we need forgiveness both personally and professionally.

One definition states that forgiveness is to "stop feeling angry or resentful toward (someone) for an offense, flaw, or mistake" (Lexico Dictionary, n.d.). Nowhere in there does it say forget, condone, justify, or continue subjecting one's self to ongoing mistreatment, so please hear us when we say that creating boundaries does not indicate a lack of forgiveness. But why forgive? In a nutshell, we think Joe's dad said it best when he would say in no uncertain terms, "Buddy, don't be bitter." Holding onto anger will produce a huge crop of bitterness, which permeates every aspect of life. We are both very justice-oriented persons, but it's really not our job to sort through whether something was malicious in intent or an unintentional mistake, whether someone deserves forgiveness, or even if someone deserves some type of consequence. The point is that holding onto the anger only serves to create a toxicity within each of us. The Mayo Clinic Staff (n.d.) says that forgiveness can lead to improved health and peace of mind and lead to:

- Healthier relationships
- Improved mental health

- Less anxiety, stress, and hostility
- Lower blood pressure
- Fewer symptoms of depression
- A stronger immune system
- Improved heart health
- Improved self-esteem

All in all, forgiveness needs to be included in our personal and professional self-care toolkit. "Forgiveness is not always easy. At times, it feels more painful than the wound we suffered, to forgive the one that inflicted it. And yet, there is no peace without forgiveness" (Williamson, 2013). Forgiveness isn't a gift to the transgressor; it's a gift for yourself.

Let's not forget forgiving ourselves, as well. More often than not, we are our own worst critics. Being harsh with ourselves seems to come easily when we feel like we're falling short in some aspect of life. Give yourself grace when you feel like you haven't been operating up to your measuring stick. Grace is defined by Merriam-Webster online as "disposition to or an act or instance of kindness, courtesy, or clemency; a temporary exemption." Please note the word temporary. Giving yourself grace doesn't mean you've resigned yourself to a pattern of operating subpar, but instead you're giving yourself a break for being human. After you've extended yourself grace, then let the feelings of defeat or failure or whatever go. Anything less signifies a lack of self-forgiveness.

If you feel like at the root of your feelings is that you've wronged another person, then go do the right thing! You'll feel better for seeking forgiveness, and often, the other person will be receptive and feel better, too. Many schools are beginning to institute restorative practices for students who have exercised a poor attitude or behavior. As adults, we should seek to do the same to keep relationships with self and others healthy while simultaneously bolstering the health of our workplace culture.

The Time for Impact Is Now—The "Who" Is You

It breaks us every time we hear of another educator who began their careers passionate about their calling only to find themselves disillusioned and miserable in what has become a daily grind. This is exactly why we've included a chapter outlining professional self-care strategies. Once again revisiting Chapter 3, we have no control over other people…not our students, not the parents, not our administration, not our coworkers, not the policy makers, no one except for ourselves. Do not be disheartened; rather, be empowered. We are not living in isolation where personal self-care is easily implemented and that's that; we have many external forces to contend with, our workplace being one of the primary ones. It's time for each of us to take the lead with our self-care, which includes how we equip ourselves to step into our workplace. In doing so, we can begin the steep climb to fundamentally redesigning toxic cultures where shame, blame, and indifference have been prevalent. Brown (2012) suggests:

> In an organizational culture where respect and the dignity of individuals are held as the highest values, shame and blame don't work as management styles. There is no leading by fear. Empathy is a valued asset, accountability is an expectation rather than an exception, and the primal human need for belonging is not used as leverage and social control. We can't control the behavior of individuals, however, we can cultivate organizational cultures where behaviors are not tolerated and people are held accountable for protecting what matters most: human beings.

The trap we can easily fall into is to say WE are not contributing to this problem; therefore, it's someone else's problem. If everyone is looking around and waiting for someone else to fix things, we will all be standing around staring at each other and nothing will change. However, if we take a step back and reflect, we can see that that attitude right there is full of blame and lacking any semblance of responsibility or accountability. Take it a step further, many of us were reared in a generation of fear and shame methodology. It was common practice in classrooms, on ball fields, and even for some at home, so naturally it can find its way into our daily operations disguised as effective management for maintaining control or as motivation for better outcomes. The whole direction of this conversation feels terrible, but we're keeping it real because we need to understand that toxic environments don't happen overnight. We can keep blaming. We can keep pointing out others' weaknesses. Or, we can begin exercising our strengths to break old patterns. WE can intentionally choose every single day to contribute to the solution. How? Let's look at some ideas to bring our intentions for contributing to change into focus:

1. *Be a leader, not a follower.* Have you ever said this to the kids in your charge, or maybe you remember it being said to you as a youngster? We have, but somewhere into adulthood many of us choose to allow others to do all the leading. Being a leader isn't about obtaining a certain job title or climbing into a position of power. It also doesn't mean that you're bucking against the chain of authority or management systems in place. Being a leader involves self-definition. It's about taking the wheel of your life and doing the steering; you determine your steps, your attitude, your actions, your reactions, and in doing so, you're putting out into the world what you hope to receive in return. Van der Kolk (2014) expands on four fundamental truths:

> (1) our capacity to destroy one another is matched by our capacity to heal one another. Restoring relationships and community is central to restoring well-being; (2) language gives us the power

> to change ourselves and others by communicating our experiences, helping us to define what we know, and finding a common sense of meaning; (3) we have the ability to regulate our own physiology, including some of the so-called involuntary functions of the body and brain, through such basic activities as breathing, moving, and touching; and (4) *we can change social conditions to create environments in which children and adults can feel safe and where they can thrive* (emphasis ours). When we ignore these quintessential dimensions of humanity, we deprive people of ways to heal from trauma and restore their autonomy. Being a patient, rather than a participant in one's healing process, separates suffering people from their community and alienates them from an inner sense of self.

We each need to take the lead in reconnecting the dots of the community within our workplaces. Further, Kouzes and Posner state, "By asking ourselves how we want to be remembered, we plant the seeds for living our lives as if we matter. By living each day as if we matter, we offer up our own unique legacy. By offering up our own unique legacy, we make the world we inhabit a better place than we found it" (2006). You may feel at first like you are the only one, but be that one.

Our children attend an elementary school that encourages leadership, and at the end of the school year, students voted for classmates for the "Be the One" award recognizing kindness and leadership. Two of our daughters were the recipients of this award; we want to be like them. In a world that feels nothing but cutthroat at times, that says we are each other's opposition or competition, we want to be that person who says kindness is not weakness and leadership is being a positive contributor to the whole. We don't want to resign ourselves to the trend of negativity or a culture divided, but instead be champions for finding good in people and in life.

We also want to be like our other grade school-aged daughter who did not win the award. She celebrated with those who did win, understanding that we don't always receive accolades for doing the right thing, but she is committed to doing the right thing anyway. Caine stated at one of her leadership events, "To build a strong team, you must see someone else's strength as a compliment to your weakness, not a threat to your position or authority" (2016). Creating an atmosphere that is non-threatening and beckons success from its inhabitants only serves to create a tension-free zone emotionally conducive to people thriving instead of merely surviving.

2. *Enhance the creation of your vision by defining your legacy.* Education is a unique profession. In this profession, one has the capacity to have such a direct, profound influence on the trajectory of not just one life, but many lives, over the span of a school year or maybe even multiple school years if you happen to have that opportunity with certain students. You step into a million different stories, some full of hope, others unfathomable, but in all of it you want to make a difference. Maybe therein lies one of the roots of our fatigue. Unlike other professions where you often see the culmination of your efforts, in education you are pouring out of yourself every day in faith. You are a seed planter, expectant and hopeful there will be fruit, but some days you wonder. Is it worth it? Does it matter? Sure, we get glimpses throughout the year, but when you face the hard, the really, really hard, it can feel like chasing the wind. Joe has felt and wondered these things, and still does sometimes. If you've felt and wondered the same thing, we'd like to share with you a

message Joe received from a former student on May 17, 2018 via Facebook Messenger (another time when social media worked for good!):

> Mr. Hendershott,
>
> Were you once a principal at EHS in Elyria, Ohio? If so, I just wanted to thank you for helping me. You might not remember me, but you handed me my diploma back in 2002. I had a baby back then and I came really close to screwing up both of our futures, but you had my back. Well anyways, if this is the Mr. Hendershott I knew, I just thought it would be really cool to tell you my daughter is going to a be senior at EHS next year! She is a consistent High Honor Roll Student. She is in all honors classes and is a college student as well. She was also recently inducted into the National Honor Society. She's pretty amazing. And the 16-year-old mom you helped graduate from high school received her BSN last year and is currently working on her master's degree. She's going to be a Family Nurse Practitioner. I know this message was random. I just finished writing a paper that had me reflecting on some things. Katie

Joe explains, "I was the principal for freshman when I first encountered Katie. I say encounter because we didn't actually meet since she was brought to my office unconscious. She openly shares now that she was struggling with a lot of things and made some bad choices with substances as a way of self-medicating. We got Katie some help and headed in the right direction, and then she became pregnant during her sophomore year. While some would argue that this might be the time to move on, I just couldn't bring myself to throw my hands up and give up on her, and neither could others in the district. She had made such great strides. Fast forward a couple years and hard work later, and Katie's mom took a picture of me with Katie the night of her graduation. Katie wondered in her message to me in 2018 if I even remembered her. What she didn't know was that I had kept that picture of us at graduation displayed at every single job I'd had since leaving that high school as a reminder and inspiration to not give up, even in the bleakest of situations. I've needed that reminder over and over again when I've become tired or lost sight of my vision for who I am and what I'm fighting for as a professional. When Katie chose to reach out all these years later, she unknowingly inspired me again in a new way. She reminded me once again to never give up, but she also showed me that not only does it matter for the one, it matters for the generations to come."

We are not sharing Katie's message as a pat on Joe's back; it's a pat on your back. Every one of you has a Katie you may or may not know about, but friend, trust that there is. There were boys and girls who are now men and women looking fondly back on who you were to them in their early years. There are children in your midst today that will be your Katie tomorrow. As we've gone through the chapters of this book, we've encouraged you to consider your hope and vision for yourself both personally and professionally. Why? Because one of the best ways we can take care of ourselves is to not lose sight of who we want to be, and sometimes that can become lost in the middle of the mess and stress. The fatigue comes when we can't remember who and what we're fighting for and why.

One of Joe's very first assignments in his doctoral work was to write a leadership legacy statement. He was instructed to consider what his legacy would look like at the end of his career. One of the biggest lessons he learned through this assignment was that defining the hope for his legacy allowed him to sharpen his vision for the journey between here and there. He also learned that it's fluid. What he would have written just out of college about his legacy has certainly evolved with time and experience, but the foundational hope to make an impact is still there. Joe's career has taken lots of twists and turns, but at the heart of this father, teacher, coach, and administrator has been and always will be to empower young people to be the best they can be; to hope, to dream, and to believe they are important in this world. Over the last several years, that vision has evolved further as together we have extended our heart's desire to empowering educators serving young people to be the best they can be; to hope, to dream, to rediscover lost passion, and to believe you are important and what you're doing matters, even if you haven't heard from your Katie yet. We are confident that you will.

Professional Self-Care Strategies At-a-Glance

- Be a trusted colleague.
- Avoid negative interactions.
- You can't care too much.
- Assume competence.
- Utilize your gifts.
- Be a mentor—find a mentor.
- Forgive.

Action steps:

- Be a leader.
- Define your legacy.

Reading, Reflection, and Discussion Points

1. What are the strengths in your organization's functioning? What are its challenge points?
2. Please describe your ideal work environment in detail. Be as specific as possible with the various aspects of your organization's functioning.

3. What are your strengths as a trusted colleague? What are your challenge points?
4. Do you feel your organization as a whole tends to have a positive or negative culture? What kind of contribution do you regularly make to this culture?
5. On a scale of 1 to 5 with 5 being considered the highest, how would your colleagues rate you on the following:
    - Conveys an open door policy. ______
    - Listens to hear instead of listening to fix. ______
    - Does not minimize others' feelings. ______
    - Attunes to the needs of others. ______
6. What is your attitude or response if someone delegates a task to you?
7. How do you feel when you have to entrust a task to another person?

    Group discussion: As a team, do we cultivate an air of confidence in working together? Is there an assumption of competence that is mutual, whether we are the delegator or the one delegated to?
8. What is something—a talent, a hobby, a skill, a passion—that your coworkers and/or your students might enjoy knowing about you?
9. How might you benefit from having a mentor?
10. What can you share as a mentor to a colleague?
11. How do you think extending grace and forgiveness in the workplace would impact the culture? How would it impact you personally?
12. How would you define yourself as a leader?

Professional Self-Care Assignment

Take some time to revisit how your hope and vision for yourself both personally and professionally has evolved since the beginning of this book. With this in mind, write your leadership legacy statement (Hint: Your journal would be a great spot to write this out!). Keep it near to you, revisit it often, and revise as your journey unfolds.

Group activity: Share your leadership legacy statements with the group. As a group, develop a legacy statement for your professional setting as a whole. Consider creating something (a document, artwork, bulletin board, etc.) where you can be reminded and inspired by your collaborative vision.

References

Attunement. (n.d.). In Alleydog.com's online glossary. Retrieved June 2019, from https://www.alleydog.com/glossary/definition-cit.php?term=Attunement

Brown, C. B. (2012). *Daring greatly: How the courage to be vulnerable transforms the way we live, love, parent, and lead*. New York, NY: Gotham.

Carter, S. B. (2012). Emotions are contagious—choose your company wisely. Retrieved June 2019, from https://www.psychologytoday.com/us/blog/high-octane-women/201210/emotions-are-contagious-choose-your-company-wisely

Caine, C. (2016, February 5). To build a strong team you must see someone else's strength as a complement to your weakness not a threat to your position or authority (Twitter Post). Retrieved August 2019, from https://twitter.com/christinecaine/status/695680295236870144?lang=en

Covey, S. R. (2004). *The 7 habits of highly effective people: Restoring the character ethic*. New York, NY: Free Press.

Kouzes, J. & Posner, B. (2006). *A leader's legacy*. San Francisco, CA: Jossey-Bass.

Lexico Dictionary. (n.d.). Retrieved August 2019, from https://www.lexico.com/en/definition/forgive.

Mayo Clinic Staff. (n.d.). Forgiveness: Letting go of grudges and bitterness. Retrieved June 2019, from https://www.mayoclinic.org/healthy-lifestyle/adult-health/in-depth/forgiveness/art-20047692

Melvill, H. (1855). *The golden lectures*. London, England: James Paul.

Merriam-Webster Online Dictionary. (n.d.). Retrieved August 2019, from https://www.merriam-webster.com/dictionary/grace

Mother Teresa Quotes. (n.d.). BrainyQuote.com. Retrieved October 2019, from https://www.brainyquote.com/quotes/mother_teresa_107032

Perry, B. D., & Szalavitz, M. (2008). *The boy who was raised as a dog: And other stories from a child psychiatrist's notebook: What traumatized children can teach us about loss, love, and healing*. New York, NY: Basic Books.

Podolsky, A., Kini, T., Bishop, J., & Darling-Hammond, L. (2016). *Solving the teacher shortage: How to attract and retain excellent educators*. Retrieved August 2019, from https://learningpolicyinstitute.org/product/solving-teacher-shortage.

Schawbel, D. (2017). Brene Brown: Why human connection will bring us closer together. Retrieved June 2019, from https://www.forbes.com/sites/danschawbel/2017/09/12/brene-brown-why-human-connection-will-bring-us-closer-together/#2d29e4e32f06

Szalavitz, M., & Perry, B. D. (2010). *Born for love: Why empathy is essential and endangered*. New York, NY: William Morrow.

Valerio, N. (2019). Viral Facebook post urges people to rethink self-care. Retrieved April 2019, from https://www.flare.com/identity/self-care-new-zealand-muslim-attack/

Van der Kolk, B. A. (2014). *The body keeps the score: Brain, mind, and body in the healing of trauma*. New York, NY: Viking.

Williamson, M. (2013). *Illuminata: Thoughts, prayers, rites of passage*, New York, NY: Random House.

Wood, W. (2016). Is it important for athletes to have fun? Retrieved June 2019, from https://www.psychologytoday.com/us/blog/the-coach-athlete-relationship/201605/is-it-important-athletes-have-fun

Concluding Thoughts

A simple online search of the phrase "secure identity" generates a plethora of results about how to protect one's personal information from identity theft. One of the most vital pieces of self-care needs to be the protection of our personal identities; the essence of who we are and what we hope to become. Our search for wholeness is every bit as much for our mental well-being as our physical, so the path to self-discovery and self-definition is imperative. Our identities anchor us within the whole of this world, but an anchor can be defined in two ways: It can be a heavy weight that restricts motion, or it can provide a sense of strength, security, and support. Know who you are, and then resolve to strengthen any aspect of your self-care that may be compromised in a way that keeps you from being who you are and following the path you want to follow. Roth and Fitzgerald wrote, "For what it's worth: it's never too late or, in my case, too early to be whoever you want to be. There's no time limit, stop whenever you want. You can change or stay the same, there are no rules to this thing. We can make the best or the worst of it. I hope you make the best of it. And I hope you see things that startle you. I hope you feel things you never felt before. I hope you meet people with a different point of view. I hope you live a life you're proud of. If you find that you're not, I hope you have the courage to start all over again" (2008).

As people, as educators, most everything we do is a product of our identity. Occasionally, life throws us some adversities that add other layers to our identity we didn't necessarily want to own. However, we hope throughout the pages of this book you've come to a place of understanding that we can reconcile those very experiences that feel like a burden into a part of our identity that convicts, strengthens, and moves us with passion toward action. When we acknowledge how our own personal adversities might be impeding our attempts at self-care, we can redesign those barriers into pathways leading to personal wellness. Our identity becomes a sum of experiences and a continued journey toward further self-discovery rather than an internal battle that hinders and handcuffs us to mediocrity. We can proceed with a boldness and confidence into this calling to impact the lives of our students, knowing full well that the areas we have previously viewed as weaknesses or wounds too deep to heal may well be the avenues best taken to authentic connections with our students as well as within our professional communities and relationships.

Acknowledging our wounds can turn them from obstacles to stepping stones toward implementing effective self-care. This, in turn, can rejuvenate our sense of self and purpose, which assists us in contributing to healthy work cultures and establishing a vision for our legacy. The hardest parts of our stories may well be the lifeline and bridge to hope for another. And ultimately, embracing who we are, envisioning who we are becoming, and stepping into the trenches of education every day is like tossing a pebble into the vastness of humanity to see just how far the ripples can go. Press on, Warrior of Hope. You got this.

Reference

Roth, E., & Fitzgerald, F. S. (2008). *The curious case of Benjamin button: Story to screenplay*. New York, NY: Scribner.

Appendix

Hope 4 The Wounded, LLC

TRAUMA INDICATOR CHART

NAME: ____________________ ACTION

DATE: ____________________ PLAN: ____________________

GRADE: ____________________ ____________________

AGE: ____________________ ____________________

PHYSICAL:	Abuse (Sexual, Physical) ___ Drug/Alcohol Usage ___ Anger ___ Violence ___ Absence of Parent(s) ___ Lack of Support ___ Previous Incarceration (Self) ___ Parent(s) Incarcerated ___ Bullying/Bullied ___ Human Trafficking ___ Neglect ___ Other ____________________
EMOTIONAL:	Grief ___ Adoption ___ Foster Care ___ Verbal Abuse ___ Hopelessness ___ Parents Divorce/Separation ___ Lack of Academic/Life Success ___ Fear ___ Military/Deployed ___ Loss of Home ___ Teen Parent (self/family member) ___ Witness Shooting ___ Witness Accident ___ Witness Violence ___ Immigrant ___ Suicidal ___ Other Stressful Event/Situation ____________
MEDICAL:	Anxiety ___ Depression ___ Obsessive/Compulsive ___ Malnutrition ___ Self-Harm ___ Eating Disorder ___ Chronic Illness ___ Terminal Illness ___ Critical Illness (self/family) ___ Major Medical Needs/Interventions ___ Other __________
SOCIAL:	Reactive Attachment Disorder (also medical) ___ Low Self-Esteem ___ Withdrawn ___ Poverty ___ Isolation or Exclusion ___ Lack of Healthy Boundaries ___ Trust Issues __ Lying ___ Negative Attitude about Self/Others ___ Other ____________________

**This is not an exhaustive list but rather a starting point for identifying children beyond at-risk and the possible barriers to their academic & life success. Some indicators may fall into multiple categories. This list is for informational purposes only. Please utilize your organization's resources and protocol for implementing interventions and referring for professional mental health services, when necessary.

NOTES:

www.hope4thewounded.org

Taylor & Francis eBooks

www.taylorfrancis.com

A single destination for eBooks from Taylor & Francis with increased functionality and an improved user experience to meet the needs of our customers.

90,000+ eBooks of award-winning academic content in Humanities, Social Science, Science, Technology, Engineering, and Medical written by a global network of editors and authors.

TAYLOR & FRANCIS EBOOKS OFFERS:

A streamlined experience for our library customers

A single point of discovery for all of our eBook content

Improved search and discovery of content at both book and chapter level

REQUEST A FREE TRIAL

support@taylorfrancis.com